VASTU IN 10 SIMPLE LESSONS

VASTU

IN 10 SIMPLE LESSONS

Bilkis Whelan

WATSON-GUPTILL PUBLICATIONS
New York

First edition for the United States in 2002 by
Watson-Guptill Publications,
a division of BPI Communications Inc.,
770 Broadway, New York, NY 10003

Conceived, designed, and produced by

THE IVY PRESS LIMITED

The Old Candlemakers, West Street, Lewes, East Sussex BN7 2NZ

The moral right of the author has been asserted.

CREATIVE DIRECTOR Peter Bridgewater
PUBLISHER Sophie Collins
EDITORIAL DIRECTOR Steve Luck
DESIGN MANAGER Tony Seddon
DESIGNER Jane Lanaway
PROJECT EDITOR Georga Godwin
PICTURE RESEARCH Vanessa Fletcher, Trudi Valter
ILLUSTRATORS Richard Constable, Ivan Hissey,
Andrew Kulman, Tony Simpson, Colleen Waugh
PHOTOGRAPHY Ian Parsons

Library of Congress Control Number: 2001096615
ISBN 0-7641-1862-5

Reproduction and printing in China by
Hong Kong Graphics and Printing Ltd.

CONTENTS

1

HISTORY OF VASTU

Despite colonization, cultural traditions have been maintained in India. As more and more Indians have settled around the world, they have taken their culture, food, and beliefs along with them.

Vastu is the Hindi (one of the Indian languages) word for abode and *Shastra* means knowledge. These words describe a systematic approach to building and design that helps us live in harmony with our environment. Vastu Shastra has its origins in Hindu traditions and has been used for many centuries. Vastu Shastra is mentioned in the *Ramayana* and the *Mahabharata,* two of India's classic epics; the rituals of Vastu Shastra are described in ancient texts such as the *Sutras, Vedas,* and *Puranas.* Although it is rooted in Hindu culture, Vastu Shastra can be used by anyone—whether they belong to a religion or not.

The concepts of Vastu Shastra evolved during the sixth or seventh centuries, but it was in the tenth or eleventh centuries that the two Vastu Shastra books, titled *Manasara* and *Mayamatam,* were written. The earliest known Vastu Shastra practitioners were the the builders/architects Vishwakarma and Maya.

According to the *Vedas,* each person has four purposes in life. The first is *kama,* meaning emotional and sensual pleasure without causing pain. The second is *artha,* meaning our materialistic wishes and the actions that make everyday life more enjoyable. The third is *dharma,* meaning doing our duty—to ourselves, to our family, and to society. The fourth purpose, the most important, is *moksha,* which deals with our need for spiritual growth, our liberation from material needs, and our journey toward *nirvana,* or enlightenment. When we achieve *moksha,* we escape from the cycle of birth and death and are truly liberated. Everyday life is an essential ingredient in achieving *moksha* and therefore the house plays an important role in helping us to achieve our goal and purpose in life.

above *"Om" is the most sacred of all Hindu syllables and is chanted both at the beginning and end of all prayers.*

left *A Hindu sadhu, religious man, sits outside an ornate temple. He is conducting a ceremony using sacred fire.*

THE AIMS OF VASTU SHASTRA

In its most complex form, Vastu Shastra sets out the designs and dimensions to be used for all kinds of buildings. These were dictated by the social status of the people who would use the building—whether it was a palace for a king, a temple for a priest, a camp for a warrior, or a home for a laborer. Vastu Shastra aimed to create a congenial environment for each and every person, of each and every stratum of society, so that they could live in true harmony with nature and the cosmic forces. While the acquisition of wealth is all too frequently the most important objective of many people in today's society, the principles of Vastu Shastra regard wealth creation as a secondary priority, although increased wealth can come about as a result of fulfilling the prime objective of living in harmony with the environment.

The environment, the climate, as well as the plot of land upon which the house was to be built had a very strong influence on Vastu Shastra designs; different designs were used for people living in, say, Rajasthan in northern India to those used for people living in Kerala in southern India. The variations were slight, perhaps seemingly insignificant to an outsider, but nonetheless necessary. Whatever the differences, however, the fundamental principles were always maintained and one of the basic aims of Vastu Shastra —to provide to each a comfortable home—has remained most important. The creation of a home that could bestow peace of mind and become one of the cornerstones of a blissful, although perhaps hard-working, life was always the intent behind Vastu Shastra. It is a fundamental belief that this goal can be brought about by enhancing the positive cosmic energies, and neutralizing negative energies.

above *Lord Brahma is the supreme god, and is believed to be the creator of the universe. He is represented here as a four-headed man.*

THE VEDAS

Vedas comprised the sacred book that was the first text to be heard, taught, and learned in India. They are a collection of hymns or sacred songs. Veda literally means sacred knowledge or wisdom. There are four kinds of Vedas.
• Rig Veda teaches and informs.
• Yajur Veda teaches karma and how one should behave.
• Sama Veda tells us about worship
• Atharva Veda is a collection of religious hymns and their explanations.

The Hindu religion is based on the holy books of the four Vedas, the Upanishads, and the epics like the Ramayanas, the Mahabharatas, as well as the sacred Hindu book, known as the Bhagwad Gita.

THE STORY OF THE DEMON

According to mythology, Lord Shiva was fighting with Andhhakarusan. It was hot, the battle was long and tiring, and as the fight continued both started to sweat profusely. A bead of Lord Shiva's sweat dripped to the ground and slowly formed into the shape of a huge and terrible demon. The demon started to eat everything in sight—just as a swarm of locusts strips vegetation—but he could not stop, he was still hungry for more. Lord Shiva saw that this demon, with his awesome strength, posed such a threat to mankind, and even to the gods themselves, that his evil power had somehow to be tamed or contained. The gods united together to conquer the demon; they cast him to the ground with his face down and his head in the northeast. His body was spread out with his feet in the southwest. When they had done this, they sat on him to contain him and control his destructive powers.

But this was not enough; they had to find a way of keeping him satisfied and thus under control. They wanted to appease him, so they told him that he could receive and eat all of the offerings that, from this point, would be required at the construction of every building. But they still let him retain the ability to punish anyone who mistreated him, ignored him, or troubled him, or broke the laws in any way.

This demon is the Purusha or the cosmic man. The Purusha is believed to be present in every home, which is the Purusha's body. One of the first steps in Vastu Shastra is to divide the house into grids (squares); each grid has a location, which is ruled by a deity who presses down on the Purusha to contain him. At each stage of construction, the blessings of the divinity of that sector are invoked, by chanting mantras. It is necessary to appease the deities themselves at various levels of construction so that they in turn are able to satisfy the Purusha in the grid of the house.

Each part of the body of the cosmic man therefore relates to a sector of the grid of the house, so the part of the body that rests there determines the function of that particular room. For instance, the head of the Purusha is always placed in the northeast and, because the head contains the brain and is the center of thought, the northeast becomes the prescribed place for worship; a *pooja* room (prayer room) should always be located in this part of the house. When a large development that contains several buildings is being constructed, the Purusha is first overlaid on the complete site, and then on each of the individual buildings contained within the site. If a temple is planned for the large development, then it would be located in the northeast of the site. The center of the grid is where the Purusha has most of his vital organs, the heart and the lungs, and this area must therefore be guarded and protected. The heart of the house is also where Lord Brahma, the four-headed Supreme Creator, resides.

above *The Vastu Purusha Mandala grid is superimposed on a site or floor plan, and the layout of the rooms in a house is then designed accordingly.*

right *The main grid that is used in the designing of a house is the Vastu Purusha Mandala grid of nine squares. The Vastu Purusha is contained entirely within this grid.*

ARM	BREAST	HEAD
LEG	HEART	BREAST
FEET	LEG	ARM

left *Each square on the grid reflects the layout of the Vastu Purusha's body. The functions of rooms relate to the body parts—the prayer room, for example, is sited in the head square, where the mind and brain are located.*

9

THE IMPORTANCE OF CREATING
HARMONY WITH THE ENVIRONMENT

The wisdom of Vastu Shastra is founded on a belief that a divine relationship is shared between the people who live in a house and the building itself. Vastu Shastra treats the building as a living entity, and the people residing there as its companions. Many people in the West can empathize with this concept of a personal relationship between an individual and their house. The house protects and shelters us from adverse weather, and from the outside world. We, in turn, should look after our house, cleaning and maintaining it. The positive environment created by the bond between home and occupier becomes an important factor in the well-being and success of the occupants.

By endeavoring to live at ease and in harmony with nature, we can help to make our everyday life more pleasant, and to make every day count. In India, although many millions of people live in poverty, they are still "house-proud." It is immaterial to them that the house, of which they are so proud, might be just a little room shared by a big family. They accept the importance of their bond with their home, and do everything that they can to maintain and nurture it.

The environment in which each individual lives is important in Vastu Shastra and the location of the house, the shape and size of the plot, the location of each room, the function of each room, the location and size of windows, the location and size of doors, the color schemes, and even the material used in the construction has a rule that governs it. Traditionally, to break any of these rules or laws was seen as working against nature, although in today's world we sometimes have little choice in the matter. Since the house is an extension of the owner and is also a dwelling of the gods, it is believed that a positive environment will keep the gods happy and also enhance the good fortune of its residents.

below A plant will add color and fragrance to any corner of the house or garden.

above The colors in a room are chosen according to the function of the room— bright colors in living and eating areas, while more subdued colors are used for resting and sleeping areas.

In Hindu culture, each religious ritual is geared to ensure the enhancement of positive energies and to seek blessings from the various gods. In the past, any natural calamity was seen as a manifestation of the anger of the gods. For Hindus it is therefore vital to pray and give religious offerings so as to appease the gods, seek their approval, and therefore prevent any kind of "punishment." In India, it is quite normal to have a little corner in the home for religious icons and prayer. It is also quite normal for each person in the household to start the day by paying homage to their god. Being successful is considered to be a result of having the "gods smiling at you," and living in harmony with nature.

Vastu Shastra also incorporates the use of symbols to create a positive force, or energy. Two of the most sacred symbols, *Swastika* and *Om* are widely used. *Swastika* means, "all well." Despite its misuse in Europe during the first half of the twentieth century, the swastika is used to seek blessings in homes and offices and is believed to ensure the smooth progress of a project. It is also believed to be a sign that brings prosperity, wealth, and good fortune. This symbol is drawn on business documents and sometimes even bridal clothes for luck. It is also painted on thresholds and walls to energize homes. Some people wear it as a talisman to ward off evil, despair, and darkness. Its vertical lines indicate self and the horizontal lines indicate the universe. The four sides point to the four cardinal directions. The swastika symbol is the replica of Lord Vishnu himself, normally shown in red or saffron colors.

Om can also be written as *AUM*. It is the visual depiction of the cosmic sound from which all matter originates. All invocations, or mantras, start with this word—including those recited at any religious occasion. This motif is used to decorate temples, doorways, ceremonial clothes, and even account books, and to enhance the auspicious energies in the house.

below It is normal Hindu practice to "dress" the gods, to make offerings of food, fresh flowers, and to burn incense to honor the gods.

above A collection of religious symbols, shapes and designs, considered auspicious when used in homes.

above This sacred symbol is an emblem of the Sun, and should not be confused with the Nazi swastika.

above This is "Om" written in Hindi. This auspicious sign adorns the entrance of many homes and offices to bring good luck.

THE FORCES OF NATURE

Vastu Shastra emphasizes the importance of attracting the positive energies, or "prana" (the life-giving force), from the land. In China prana is known as "chi;" in Japan it is called "ki." Without prana or chi or ki, life would not exist; it is the all-pervading cosmic force that animates all creation. It is found in food, water, and air. It flows through the body, and sickness and ill health will result wherever it is blocked. Our thought processes are considered to be the most refined action of prana. There can be no life or thought without it.

Prana has to flow through the living space without any impediments—hence the house should always be clutter-free to encourage its smooth progress. To attract good, positive energy to the house, it is essential that the house is kept clean, and free of dust, clutter, and dirt. A house that is full of clutter can block the smooth flow of energy and may result in sickness and ill health for family members. Vastu Shastra helps us to enhance this positive life-giving force and to neutralize the negative forces of nature.

above Clutter can block the smooth flow of energy, or prana, in a home, causing the energies to stagnate. It is far better to get rid of unwanted things.

below Well-arranged furniture that is kept to a minimum encourages a good flow of energy. It is best to keep the center of the room clear of any furniture.

KEY DIFFERENCES BETWEEN
VASTU SHASTRA AND FENG SHUI

Both Vastu Shastra and feng shui set out to achieve the same objective, despite their different origins. Vastu Shastra relates to architecture and building, and was used in India for designing palaces and temples. "Feng shui," from China, means "wind and water." Originally, feng shui was used to determine auspicious burial places, but today feng shui is mainly practiced for the living.

Both approaches emphasize the five elements; where Vastu Shastra includes wind and space but not metal and wood, feng shui does the reverse. In the practice of feng shui, the home is simply seen as a dwelling place, although many design features will depend on the owner's birth details (i.e., the birth month, day, and year), which are considered important in designing a house. Vastu Shastra, on the other hand, considers the home to be the place where the Purusha, or the cosmic man, resides and it uses universal principles as the cornerstones of house designs.

above *Feng shui is akin to Vastu Shastra, from ancient China, it to is practised to ensure living in harmony with one's environment.*

below *Feng shui and Vastu Shastra are two different beliefs and belong to two very different countries and cultures—they should not be "mixed".*

There are several different schools of feng shui—Black Hat Sect feng shui, Classical or Traditional Chinese compass feng shui, Intuitive feng shui, and Form school feng shui. In Vastu Shastra, there is only one school of belief. Feng shui groups people according to their birth year as "east" or "west," and uses this grouping to determine their good or bad directions. Vastu Shastra considers that all people have universal good and bad directions irrespective of their birth dates. One of the major differences between the two beliefs is in the treatment of the south. The Chinese tradition identifies south with fame and recognition. The Indians view it as not being the most auspicious of directions. It is the direction to which the feet of the dead are faced.

Both feng shui and Vastu Shastra use grids in the layout and design of a house, office, or garden. Feng shui has a nine-square grid known as the *lo shu*, but the grid used in Vastu Shastra can run from a single square into hundreds of squares. One of the major differences between the two is that, for Vastu Shastra, the sun's journey through the sky has a major influence on the design and allocation of rooms. The sun's movements have little importance in feng shui. Instead, energies are bounded by time—they change every two hours; noticeable changes occur every year; and major changes every twenty years. Because of these changes, homes are subject to structural review and alteration at frequent intervals. The approach to the landscape also differs between the two. In Vastu Shastra the south, west, and southwest regions of a plot should be higher or taller, and heavier than other directions, whereas in feng shui, the area of a plot behind the house should be higher than that in front of it—irrespective of where it is in relation to its compass location.

The beliefs underlying both feng shui and Vastu Shastra

right *The feng shui consultant uses a specially designed compass as a tool to design a house. The Vastu consultant, on the other hand, relies on the rising and the setting of the sun to design the layout of the house. So Vastu practitioners use a standard compass as their tool.*

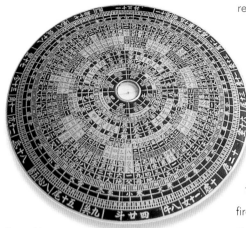

above *A Luopan is a Chinese compass that is used to determine the directions and the various formulae that might be referred to in the planning and designing of a house along feng shui lines.*

recommend that any body of water near your home should ideally be located in the front of the property since both believe that it enhances wealth. In Vastu Shastra, the flow of the water should be either from the west to the east, or from south to north. Feng shui, however, uses special water formulae, which determine the water flow according to the direction in which the property faces.

In the kitchen, feng shui considers that the orientation of the control knobs of the oven, known as the fire mouth, is the important factor while Vastu Shastra recommends facing east while cooking. In feng shui, a special compass called the *Luopan* is used to calculate directions and formulae while Vastu Shastra uses a regular compass.

Vastu Shastra and feng shui each have the same general objectives, to enable each person to live in harmony with their environment and thus to enhance their quality of life, but they approach those objectives in different ways. In the same way that five is the sum of, say two and three, or one and four, "five" will never be arrived at by adding one and two. You cannot mix the two practices—they will not harmonize; you have to choose one or the other.

above *In Vastu Shastra the northeast is considered to be the most sacred of all the directions, and is known as the "gateway to the gods."*

left *In Vastu Shastra it is important to face east whilst cooking, while in feng shui the location of the "knobs" and "controls" is considered more important.*

HISTORY OF VASTU

10

QUESTIONS & ANSWERS

Q I am confused about the difference between Shastra and Vidya. Can you explain it?

A Vastu Shastra and Vastu Vidya are the same thing—just different words that people use to describe the same concept. Vidya means "study" and Shastra means "a body of knowledge." The most frequently used term is Vastu Shastra.

Q Do you have to be a Hindu in order to practice Vastu Shastra?

A Anyone can follow Vastu Shastra principles. It is not limited to a specific religion or a particular country—it can be used anywhere and by absolutely anyone, irrespective of their religous beliefs (or lack of them). You can adopt the principles of Vastu Shastra without having to say the prayers or perform the rituals that Hindus do.

Q Is it possible to incorporate both Vastu Shastra and feng shui in the design of my new property?

A When it comes to architectural design, you cannot mix the two systems. They use totally different methodologies, and while both aim at creating harmony, mixing them would not achieve your purpose. The building or house would look different if designed along feng shui rather than Vastu Shastra principles, since the rules, formulas, elements, and grid are all aligned differently.

Q Does Lord Brahma have a presence in every house?

A People who believe in Vastu Shastra believe that Lord Brahma exists at the center of all properties. In practicing Vastu Shastra, in a purely secular way, you should at least accept that the center of your house is the focus of all energies.

Q My family and I live in a house that was not built along Vastu Shastra principles, although we are interested in incorporating them. Is it too late to do so?

A It is never too late to adopt Vastu Shastra. Ideally, it should be done by professional consultants, who will conform to any building codes and regulations. Unless you build a house from scratch, it is unlikely that you will get everything to comply with Vastu Shastra, but do what you can. Work on one room to begin with and then move on to adapt the other rooms.

Q Is having statues or pictures of Hindu gods an essential component of Vastu? If so, in which corner or my room should I place them?

A You need not have any statues or pictures of Hindu gods—it all depends on your religious beliefs. If you are so inclined, you can place some religious objects in the northeast corner of your room, but if you are not a religious person, then by all means leave that area clear.

Q Do I have to learn all the names of the various gods who govern the sectors of the house?

A Non-Hindus can quite easily practice Vastu Shastra without learning all the traditions. You don't have to know any of the names—you just need to follow the principles. The north, northeast, and east of the house are where the positive energies lie, so these areas should be sparsely furnished; the west, southwest, and northwest should contain any heavy furniture. The center of the room or house should always be clear, open, and free of furniture, because this is where Lord Brahma lives.

Q I live in a one-bedroom apartment, so I do not have a northeast room to use as a place of worship as prescribed in Vastu principles. What can I do about this?

A You can use the northeast side or corner of your main room as your place of worship. Some people are fortunate enough to live in large houses where they can have a separate room devoted to worship, but most of us have to make do with rather less space. Those people who do not practice any religion can use the northeast area for quiet thought and meditation instead.

Q Does it accord with Vastu principles to have the symbol "Om" inscribed on the floor in the center of my living room?

A "Om" is a sacred symbol and so you should respect it. Placing it on the floor is disrespectful because people can walk all over it. This symbol is normally placed above the main entrance to a house to ask for blessings on the property.

Q Which is more effective in bringing good luck—feng shui or Vastu Shastra?

A Both feng shui and Vastu Shastra attract positive energies into your life—enhancing love, happiness, prosperity, and relationships, and encouraging us to live in harmony with nature. Neither concept has been assessed scientifically, although many people follow one system or the other in the hope of improving the quality of their lives. However, you should not look for quick results from either system.

2
BASIC PRINCIPLES

We have seen that the main objective of Vastu Shastra is to help us to live in harmony with nature and the environment. Building homes according to Vastu Shastra principles requires a basic understanding of its many components, such as elements, colors, and directions.

It is an Indian belief that many energies are present in the environment. These energies, collectively called "prana," are the universal life-giving force, around which everything revolves. Prana is all-pervasive; it is present not only as energy output—for example the electricity that is produced from oil—but it is also present in the energy source—both the oil itself, and the vegetation from which, over thousands of years, the oil has been derived. Prana is also present in every organ of the body, and in the blood that courses through the veins. Prana is present in the five elements—Air, Earth, Space, Fire, and Water, which, in Hindi, are called "*panch maha bhootas*." It is essential that they remain in balance for harmony to be present in the world, and these elements are sometimes called the tools of Vastu Shastra.

Vastu Shastra takes each of the five elements and associates it with one or more rooms in a house, depending on where each room falls within the mandala, and also with specific sectors of each room belonging to a physical direction within that house. Each *maha bhoota* is also represented by a particular color, a direction, a shape, and a deity, as well as being associated with the seasons, body divisions, senses, body associations (for example, thirst, hunger, and so on)—but we will concentrate on the major components only.

below *Both the main door and the adjacent road are used to determine which way the house is "facing".*

SPACE

AIR

FIRE

WATER

EARTH

above *The "panch maha bhoota" are the five basic elements that are found all round us.*

THE FIVE ELEMENTS

AIR

Air, a mixture of nitrogen and oxygen, is an essential life-supporting element. Our health is enhanced by fresh and sweet-smelling air. It is easy to understand why air is associated with movement and restlessness; the wind is a visible demonstration of the air's prana. It has west as its cardinal direction, and all reflective surfaces, such as mirrors, glass, and polished wood, "belong" to the element. Air is represented by a crescent shape and the color gray.

To help to understand its significance, we need just to look at how we take care of our homes. We "air" them periodically to avoid having a damp or musty house that would not be conducive either to our comfort or good health. In addition to keeping our homes damp-free by throwing open the windows, we also welcome the energies of the invigorating Sun. In Vastu Shastra, air is sometimes called the "breath of the Purusha (the Cosmic Man)." Clean, fresh air is a key requisite for the health of family members living in the house or apartment.

Air is a feminine element, and is associated with the part of the body from the head to the heart. Conscience and completion are two of its attributes. The western zodiac air signs are Gemini, Libra, and Aquarius.

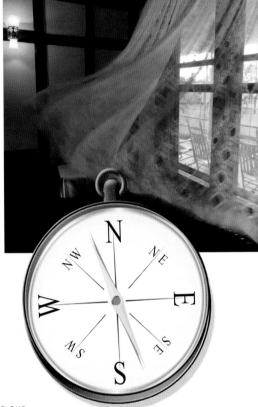

above *The northwest sector is ruled by Vayu, the god of wind. The key attributes of this direction are mobility and restlessness.*

GODS		
Direction	Indian God	Characteristic
North	Kubera	Health and wealth
Northeast	Ishanna	Purity
East	Surya	Power
Southeast	Agni	Fire
South	Yama	Justice
Southwest	Nirritti	Misery
West	Varuna	Water
Northwest	Vayu	Wind

19

FIRE

The sun is a ball of fire and a vital source of continued life on Earth. Without the heat of the sun, all life would perish. Fire is an important part of many Indian religious rituals and ceremonies. Fire is masculine and belongs to the east sector of the house or the plot. The element is, perhaps naturally, associated with the color red, and with a triangle shape. The body's fire zone runs from the heart to the navel and its attributes are passion and valor. The western zodiac fire signs are Aries, Leo, and Sagittarius.

above *Hindus believe that their sins are forgiven if they bathe in the holy river Ganges at least once during their lifetime.*

above *A Hindu religious "pundit" conducts a "pooja" (prayer), a religious ritual, with the help of "agni," or fire.*

WATER

Since 90 percent of the human body is water, it is easy to see why it is essential to our growth and survival. Water is cleansing, cooling, and life-preserving. The water element is considered to be masculine, and is represented by the north direction and the shape of a circle, which itself represents fullness. Its associated color is blue. Water plays an important part in many religious rituals, as a means of purifying and cleansing. For many Indians, the Ganges is a sacred river and they aspire to cleanse their sins by immersing themselves in its holy waters at least once in their lifetime. The body's water zone runs from the navel to the knees. Its attributes include coolness and fluidity. The western zodiac water signs are Cancer, Scorpio, and Pisces.

EARTH

Earth is the element in which much of our food is grown—without earth, most plants would not live and neither would we. Earth is feminine and belongs to the south direction of the house or plot; it is associated with a square shape and the color yellow. In the body, earth takes over from the knees to the feet, and has attributes of solidity, dependability, and single-mindeness. Its western zodiac signs are Taurus, Virgo, and Capricorn.

above *Space has no specific directional associations, and lacks gender and color. It is nonetheless one of the five important elements.*

SPACE

We are surrounded by space. Sometimes referred to as "sky" or "ether," space is an all-encompassing element, not to be confused with air, which has a chemical composition. Space has its own mystique; it has no gender, has no directional association, and is also colorless. Its bodily attributes include desire and shame.

Each element has to be in balance—-both in itself and with the the elements. No single element should predominate in a room or house. Would we be comfortable living in a room absolutely full of furniture or, on the other hand, in a room completely devoid of furniture? Probably not. We must look for balance.

below *Lush fertile earth is important for a good crop. It is also an indicator of the presence of positive energies.*

21

THE IMPORTANT COLORS

Colors in Vastu Shastra are associated with energy and emotions, improving the feeling of space and light and enhancing a mood.

Indian clothes and homes exude color and vibrancy—the reds, oranges, and greens are all eye-catching. The annual festival of colors, called "Holi" seeks the blessing of a good harvest with bonfires lit to cleanse the air of evil spirits. On the morning of Holi, people play with powdered colors and colored water, creating mayhem as they throw colors at one another.

Children love bright colors. McDonald's restaurants, for example, are red and yellow, which act as a magnet for children of all ages. Even in India, a child's idea of a day out is a burger at the Golden Arches— albeit a hamburger without beef! (In India, the cow is a sacred animal and has legal protection so it cannot be eaten).

While adults also love color, their idea of an ideal restaurant is quite different. They look for a décor of paler shades, subdued lighting, and so on —all enhancing softer and relaxing energies.

In Vastu Shastra, the important colors are violet, white, blue, green, yellow, orange, and red. Each color denotes an emotion; sometimes two colors "share" an emotion—blue and green, for example, are considered to be colors that calm and soothe, while red is considered to be passionate and to increase desire—a good color for a bedroom. As seen earlier, some colors also are associated with elements—such as yellow with earth.

above *The Indian festivity "holi", when people play with powdered colors, is a joyful celebration of a new season.*

right *The Taj Mahal is a mausoleum built by the Mughal ruler Shah Jahan as a tribute to his wife Mumtaz Mahal.*

VIOLET

Violet stimulates contemplation and meditation and is therefore a good color for a room where one wants to pray, meditate, or just be silent.

WHITE

In India, white is associated with mourning and death, and is the preferred color at death ceremonies or funerals. Widowed men and women wear white—often for the rest of their lives. A house that is painted white all over is therefore not desirable—the Prime Minister's official residence in New Delhi is a shade of red (no Washington-style White House here!). If you have no choice over the color of your house, or the house is already painted white, then use spot colors on the fence, or for the doors or windows to relieve the starkness and symbolism of white. If the inside of the house is painted white, then colors can be used in curtains, rugs, vases, pictures, cushion covers, throws, and so on.

RED

Indians associate red with celebrations and auspicious events. It is believed to protect against evil. It was the custom, in the past, to paint threshold areas red, to ward off the evil spirits. Red is the color of passion and desire, and brings an ambience of warmth and elegance wherever it is used. Indian brides wear red, with gold adornment, as the color for their wedding costume. The Hindu bride will wear a "sindoor" or "tilak" or "bindi;" this is a small red dot, which is applied by powder (or nowadays often a sticker) on the forehead. In the past, the bindi was worn only to denote marital status; today it is often used as decoration.

above *Throw cushions can be used to bring one of the five elements into the room, by introducing both specific colors and shapes.*

far right *A Hindu bride wears red and gold finery on her wedding day in order to guard against evil and bring good fortune.*

above *Peaceful contemplation and meditation are encouraged by the color violet.*

23

above *Tall windows provide this room with plenty of air and light, and also contribute to feelings of space.*

left *A well-placed lamp alleviates dark corners and is a great mood enhancer. Yellow lamps are recommended for studies and libraries.*

GREEN

Green signifies harmony, fertility, and harvest. It is the preferred color for bedrooms. In India, married women used to wear green glass bangles to denote their marital status. When their husband died, they would break the glass bangles and wash the red bindi from their forehead—both symbolic gestures. The widow would then wear only white clothes, and no jewelry or gold would adorn her body.

above *Bangles are an important accessory in an Indian woman's wardrobe. They can be made of glass, plastic, silver, or gold, and their color reflects Vastu principles.*

BLUE

Blue represents serenity, tranquility, contentment, and calmness and is the favorite color for soothing the nerves.

ORANGE

Saffron (a shade of orange) is a color that represents purity and sacred fire. Hindu religious men and women wear saffron-colored robes to denote their spiritual purity. Saffron is the color used for the triangular-shaped flags that are often flown above temples and other religious places in India. The Indian national flag is a tricolor— saffron, white, and green: saffron denotes strength; white symbolizes peace; green stands for fertility.

YELLOW

Yellow stimulates the brain and represents knowledge. It is therefore the color that is recommended for studies and libraries. It is a color that denotes energy and excitement.

THE CARDINAL DIRECTIONS
AND THEIR CHARACTERISTICS

Vastu Shastra proposes that the sun affects our energies during its daily journey across the sky. During the morning hours, the sun's rays are considered to be very positive and beneficial, and it is felt to be very advantageous to have a house or building that faces east so that the rays of the early morning sun fall at the front of the house. As the day progresses, the intensity of the sun's rays increases. These powerful, devastating rays now have to be repelled, so the rooms that receive unrelenting, harsh sunlight need extra protection. It is recommended that the rooms in the south have thicker walls to counteract the heat and keep them cooler. It is also a good idea to use soothing, calming, and cooling colors in these rooms to counter some of the heat.

The four cardinal directions are north, south, east, and west and the four sub-directions are northeast, southeast, northwest, and southwest. A deity is believed to rule each of these directions and each direction also addresses a need, a hope, and a desire. Vastu Shastra proposes that the house has a definite square or rectangular shape so that all the energies can be contained inside the house.

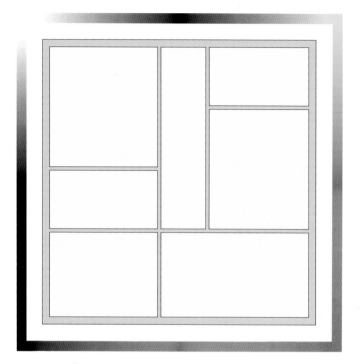

above *A house built according to Vastu principles should have the front facing the north, northeast, or east. The rear of the house should be located in the south, southwest, or west.*

right *The east is where the sun rises and the west is where the sun sets. The colors that are used in each room should therefore be chosen according to the room's relationship with the sun's journey.*

NORTH

The water element and planet Mercury, whose main attributes are knowledge, mediation, truthfulness, mental brilliance, and communication, rule the north direction of the house or property. It is associated with the color blue and the shape of the circle.

The northern direction is associated with healing powers, and Vastu Shastra principles place any medical facilities—such as a medicine cabinet—in this part of the house. North is the suggested direction to face when taking medicine.

If you have a garden and grow herbs that have healing attributes—such as cilantro for digestion, ginger for improving circulation, or aloe for soothing the skin—then the northern part of the garden is considered to be the best location.

Kubera, the god of wealth, rules the north. It is held that this is the best place to keep money, jewelry and important documents—subject to having adequate security of course. The northern direction also heralds auspicious beginnings and good and positive events; it is therefore understood to be an excellent direction to face when working, and can enhance the success of a project. It is also a good direction for building up one's spirituality, health, and wealth.

below The worktable should be free of any form of clutter in the form of paper, pens, pencils, paperclips, and so on. A cluttered desk is not considered a good workspace.

NORTH

NORTHEAST

NORTHWEST

SOUTH

WEST

right The various Vedic gods that rule each cardinal direction in a house or office.

above The purpose of a room is as important in the office as at home.

NORTHWEST

This direction is represented by the color white and is ruled by the moon, which is feminine. It is associated with the monsoon (rainy) season in India. Its attributes are mobility, activity, and restlessness. Vayu, the god of wind, rules the northwest. Vayu is believed to be the bearer of fragrances and the carrier of pollen and seeds—a rejuvenator of nature. The northwest symbolizes femininity and rules over the breasts, uterus, and stomach. The northwest is the sector that controls economic conditions and public relations, and is the direction that has an improving influence on businesses. If one starts any project either facing in this direction or using the northwest sector, it is believed that it will enhance both prosperity and luck. The northwest is another wealth-enhancing zone that benefits health and longevity.

SOUTHEAST

NORTH

NORTHWEST

NORTHEAST

The northeast, "gateway to the gods," is the source of positive cosmic energies. It is where these energies assemble before moving to other sectors. Jupiter, with its attributes of knowledge, meditation, and spiritual wisdom, rules the northeast and it is better not to have kitchens, pantries, or bathrooms in this area. Its associated color is black and its god is Ishanna, the god of purity.

Vastu Shastra contends that the cosmic energy, prana, flows two ways from the northeast—to the northwest and then to the southwest; and to the southeast and then to the southwest. While the northeast is therefore the "source" of all energies, the southwest is the "sink."

NORTHEAST

NORTHWEST

NORTHEAST

27

SOUTH

SOUTH

The south has earth as its element and yellow as its color; the square is its related shape. The attributes are smell, sound, taste, and touch. It is ruled by Mars and the god Yama, lord of justice, who decides the fate of the soul at death. The feet of the dead are pointed southward.

Anyone embarking on auspicious work should not face south, but having your back to the south builds wisdom and ends evil.

above A well-planned office or study can actually make learning easier and more enjoyable.

SOUTHEAST

SOUTHEAST

Venus rules the southeast, which is feminine and associated with love, passion, and relationships. It encompasses physical and worldly pleasures. The southeast is associated with the enhancement of virtues and personality. Agni, the god of ritual fire, rules in the southeast. Fire is an important element in religious ceremonies, including those to do with birth, marriage, and death, when it is applied from this direction and sector. When Hindus pray, they light a *diya*, an earthen lamp with a cotton wick, within this sector. At *poojas*, incense sticks are lit and placed in front of the deity's image.

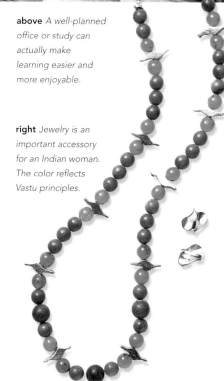

right Jewelry is an important accessory for an Indian woman. The color reflects Vastu principles.

SOUTHWEST

SOUTHWEST

This sector is associated with our ancestors. The southwest direction is ruled by the planet Uranus, and the god of misery, Nirritti. It has the least positive energies and Vastu Shastra methods are used to contain them. The southwest is also associated with dispelling fears and phobias. The color associated with this direction is black.

WEST

WEST

After its long journey, the sun sets in the west, which is associated with the element air and the color black. The planet Saturn, which is associated with grief, poverty, debt, fame, and longevity, rules the west. Varuna, the god of water, rivers, rain, and oceans, also rules here. Varuna is believed to have the power to destroy all bad spirits in the underwater world. West is associated with rain and prosperity. India is a predominantly agrarian society and any lack of rains can play havoc with its economy; an adequate and timely rainfall is essential for the well-being of the people.

EAST

The element for the east is fire, red is its color, and it is symbolized by a triangle. The sun, source of all vital energies, provider of light and heat, rules here. The sun is thought to be the source of all spiritual enlightenment. Indra, the god of power, also rules the east.

The east is associated with wealth, pleasure, fame, and recognition, and this direction is believed to sustain life and to give security and prosperity. The east has attributes of passion and strength, and is believed to advance hunger—it is linked to digestion, appetite, and goodness. East is the direction to which Hindus turn each morning for *surya namaskar*—a salutation to the sun. Facing east when undertaking any important work is a way of seeking the blessings of the sun, and is considered auspicious. It is also believed to be very good to have your head facing east while sleeping. You should face east during prayer and meditation, as it is held to be the source of all positive inspirations and energies.

EAST

above *The various elements are denoted not only by their color, but also by their shape. These are used to create balance and harmony in a room.*

below *The sun is a source of positive energies. It is vital to face east when sleeping, or when doing important work.*

above *Monsoons in India last from June to September, providing a welcome break from the harsh, unrelenting heat of the summer.*

BASIC PRINCIPLES

10

QUESTIONS
& ANSWERS

Q My house was painted white by the previous owner, but I know this is not an auspicious color in Vastu Shastra. Should I paint it another color?

A Many people choose to have white houses to achieve a clean look and because white is a good reflector of radiated heat. You don't need to alter the entire house color, but can balance the white by painting your external doors, windows and even fences and gates in brighter colors, which will negate the negative effect of white.

Q Do I have to do a *pooja* or pray at a set time if I want to follow Vastu principles?

A You can pray at any time of the day or night—or not pray, as you choose. Some religions do encourage people to pray at particular times. However, it is not necessary for you to adopt Hindu religious practices in order to follow Vastu Shastra.

Q Should I face east when I am praying, even though I am not a Hindu, to conform with Vastu principles?

A Do whatever you feel comfortable with; and if you have a religious preference, then follow that. For instance, Muslims who live to the east of Mecca (in Saudi Arabia) face west during prayer, while those living west of Mecca face east. This does not affect your ability to benefit from Vastu Shastra.

Q Is it essential to light incense sticks, or can I use candles instead in my prayer room?

A You can use either, neither, or both—it all depends on what you prefer and on your own personal beliefs. Make sure, however, that you extinguish any candles before you leave the room—safety should always be a priority.

Q My kitchen, which is in the east of the house, has blue tiles. Which is the ideal color for this direction?

A If you were starting to build a new kitchen, you might choose red tiles, but changing what you already have can be very expensive. It might also leave you with something that you don't really like. Instead, why don't you get some red "trimmings," such as pots or containers, to bring this color into the east of your house.

Q I am not an Indian or a Hindu, but can I still wear a saffron bindi/tilak on my forehead?

A A bindi, or tilak, is a dot worn in the center of the forehead. It used to be red and worn only by married Hindu women to signify that they were married. This practice has recently undergone a number of changes and the bindi has evolved from a dot to various designs and colors; it is now often worn by women of any faith, religion, or social status. We live in a secular, multicultural society, and it would not be seen as offensive for you to wear a bindi.

Q Eastern cultures seem to have different forms of energy— India has "prana," China has "chi" and Japan has "ki." What is the difference between them?

A Prana, chi, and ki all have the same meaning: life-giving energy. In feng shui, positive energy is called "sheng chi" and negative energy "shar chi." Attracting positive energy into a home is the aim of both Vastu Shastra and feng shui.

Q How do I know which of the many Hindu gods I should feature in my prayer room—or should I include them all?

A Vastu Shastra derives from Hindu belief, where there are many more gods than I mention in this book, and Hindus tend to pray to a wide range of different gods. If you want to put an image of a Hindu god in your prayer room, then choose whichever one most appeals to you. However, you don't have to be a Hindu or hold any religious belief to practice Vastu Shastra.

Q Is white a suitable color for a bedroom, according to Vastu Shastra?

A Look on the room as a blank canvas and bring in some spot colors through the use of a brightly colored duvet or bedsheets, pillows, rugs, lamps, pictures, and so on. White, although a restful color, is associated with mourning in India, so it is not an ideal color to choose, according to Vastu Shastra.

Q I would like to have a water feature with some fish in my house. In which sector should I place it?

A You can have an aquarium in the north sector, since the element that rules this sector in the Vastu Purusha Mandala grid is water. Any water feature is therefore acceptable in this area. Just make sure that the fish are always healthy and well looked after.

3

USING THE MANDALA

Long ago in India, houses were laid out around a central open square. Basic tools, such as pegs and cords, were used to lay out the foundations. A "mandala" grid was set out and the figure of the "Purusha" (Cosmic Man) was superimposed upon the grid. Measurements were crude; none of today's millimetric accuracy was possible. Natural measures were used, such as the length of the craftsman's arm. There were no compasses, and directions were determined by the positions of the sun. The sun and the moon were thought to represent the soul and mind of the Purusha.

The size of the house to be built was dependent on the social status, wealth, and position of authority of the owner. The maharajah, or king, would own the largest and most palatial property in the area. The central courtyard, was determined by the size of the house—the larger the house, the bigger the courtyard. The house design also depended on the region in which it was to be built. Different designs were used for the hot, arid climate of Rajasthan and for the wet and humid climate of Kerala. Locally available materials were used in the construction.

The practice of Vastu Shastra relied upon the expertise of four different people, who oversaw the design through to its execution; the Sthapathi, the Sutragrahin, the Vardhaki, and the Takshaka. For generations the knowledge of Vastu Shastra was passed down from father to son, with virtually no written record. The Sthapathi was the "master" builder, who was responsible for the successful design and construction of his project. He learned a wide range of subjects and skills, from math to drafting, astrology, and woodworking. He had to be healthy in mind, body, and spirit, bringing purity to all of his projects. He had three helpers: the Sutragrahin had specialized drafting skills and very good spatial awareness; the Takshaka was skilled in wood-, stone-, or metal-working; the Vardhaki was the

above *The location of the main door in a house determines the luck, health, and well-being of the people living in that house.*

far left *The Vastu Purusha, or Cosmic Man, is always placed complete in the grid with his head in the northeast and his feet in the southwest.*

painting specialist. Each one of them had been brought up learning spiritual values and had a deep knowledge and understanding of the Vedas. Today, just one person, the "Vastu Pundit," advises and works with the architect and other team leaders.

Astrology has always played a big part in the development of a property. Astrologers were consulted to see whether a site was suitable for construction and, at every stage, the astrologer was consulted to determine an auspicious time for construction of different key stages of the project.

Once built, the house and the owner were like husband and wife; they had to be compatible. There was a belief that, if the man and his house were "built for each other," then the man would prosper and find happiness in all of his endeavors. The house was a place to which the owner would return to celebrate anything happy or good in his life. It was also the place that provided him with security, warmth, and comfort and a roof over his head. The house was his "best friend," and it was his duty to look after it—he had to keep the house clean, which involved arranging for, and preparing, regular rituals and prayers so that the house was always cleansed and energized.

Today, when a new house is ready in India, it is normal for the owner to throw a housewarming party. Friends and relatives are invited and served candies and food, while prayers and rituals are performed. The priest, the architect, and the designer are also invited, as this event celebrates an important day in the life of the new owner. Each year a pooja called *"griha shanti"* (peaceful/harmonious home) is made to ask for the blessings of the gods, to bring health, wealth, happiness, and harmony to the occupants of the house.

above *The basic, but essential, tools that were required when designing, planning, and constructing a building remain the same today.*

below *In India as elsewhere weddings involve much dancing and celebrating.*

33

WHAT THE MANDALA REPRESENTS AND HOW IT IS USED

The Vastu Purusha Mandala (VPM) is a grid that contains and holds down the Purusha (Cosmic Man). It has a basic pattern of nine squares (three by three) of equal size, although it can extend to 16, 25, 64, and so on. Each square in the grid is "ruled" by its own deity, or god—the center is always ruled by Lord Brahma, known as the Supreme Creator. The name of the deity assigned to each square (and hence direction) signifies a characteristic that is based on the different positions of the sun and the moon as they each progress through the sky. The

symbolic function of the deities related to each square is to "press down" on the Purusha to control his destructive powers and prevent them from being unleashed.

The VPM grid is used to determine the layout of a building and has a major influence in its design. It is used to decide the various functions or uses of a room and even its layout. A scale representation of the property to be built is drawn on the top of the VPM grid. It is considered that the best shape for the building is a perfect square, within which the complete grid will fit. The next best shape is considered to be a rectangle.

above The phases of the moon, as judged by the amount of relected sunlight on its surface, sets the time for the religious and agricultural cycle.

right The various Vedic gods that are present in every house or office and that rule every grid and every direction of the Mandala.

Inside the mandala, the Purusha is drawn, usually lying face down, with the head in the northeast, and both feet splayed out toward the southwest. The navel, heart, and lungs are generally located in the central area of the VPM, where they will be protected by all of the other zones. During the design and construction stages and even when placing furniture, great care is taken to ensure that his navel, heart, and lungs are protected.

The sun, and its very special cosmic energy, plays a significant part in the practice of Vastu Shastra, which considers that the sun largely determines the flow of energies in the house. It follows, therefore that the sun's journey through the sky will influence the routine of people in the house, and that they can, at any time, maximize its benefits by being in the energized sectors. A house built on Vastu principles, in which the rooms are aligned as much as is practical to the ideal, is an environment in which health and harmony can grow.

above *A house that is designed according to Vastu principles is simple in shape, design, and appearance, and is in harmony with the environment.*

right *The 24 hours in a day are divided into eight subdivisions. As the sun travels from east to west activities are assigned to each subdivision.*

USING THE MANDALA		
Direction	Time	Good location for
Northeast	3-6 A.M.	Meditating
East	6-9 A.M.	Bathing
Southeast	9-12 A.M.	Cooking
South	12-3 P.M.	Siesta Room
Southwest	3-6 P.M.	Reading
West	6-9 P.M.	Eating
Northwest	9-12 P.M.	Sleeping
North	12-3 A.M.	Safe/Security

right *Dating back until at least* AD *1000, many Indian temple gateways were built in the shape of a pyramid with a square base that reflects the Vastu Purusha Mandala. Providing the base is aligned properly the pyramid is considered to be the most auspicious shape for a building, and to possess great positive energy. The triangular sides of the pyramid represent the reaching for heaven of all who enter, and are believed to magnify positive energy.*

NORTHEAST

It is very early in the morning, between 3 A.M. and 6 A.M. The Sun has not yet risen fully and there are no harmful ultra-violet emissions. The beneficial planet Jupiter, which brings both wisdom and spiritual happiness, rules the northeast. This part of the house should be fairly open or even contain empty space. It could have a balcony or terrace. Windows in this sector will bring abundant auspicious light into the house and will enhance all positive energies.

This part of the property, if built lower than the rest of the house, will gather the sun's energies before they travel into the rest of the house. Early morning is the perfect time for meditation, contemplation, or exercise.

EAST

It is between 6 A.M. and 9 A.M., and the sun has risen fully. Its rays are working for the benefit of humanity, promoting and nourishing life, and providing the energy that is essential for all life on Earth. The sun "rules" the east. The beginning of the day is the time to prepare for what lies ahead— showering, shaving, washing hair, brushing teeth. The eastern direction represents new beginnings, hope, and promise.

above *For a fit and healthy body exercise is an important part of the daily routine. The northeast sector of the house is ideal for an exercise room.*

above *Bathing and cleansing the body is an essential preparation for the new day.*

above The end of the day, when the sun is about to set on the far horizon, is the ideal time to relax and unwind.

SOUTHEAST

As the sun climbs higher in the sky, between 9 P.M. and 12 P.M., it gets stronger, radiating more powerful energy and giving more light to the southeast sector of the house. Noon is the time to prepare the midday meal. The planet Venus rules the southeast.

SOUTH

During the next three hours, from noon to 3 P.M., the Sun is at its highest in the sky and emits its strongest rays. The heat generated by the Sun can be both scorching and devastating. It is time now to take refuge from the intense heat. The planet Mars rules here.

SOUTHWEST

Between 3 P.M. and 6 P.M., as the Sun loses its intensity, is a good time to read, work, or study. The planet Uranus rules the southwest.

WEST

The time is now around 6 P.M. and the Sun is low in the sky, ready to set. The Sun now rules the western sector. The planet that rules here is Saturn. This sector is considered to be a zone for retrospection and peace.

NORTHWEST

At 9 P.M. the Sun has set and the moon rules the northwest part of the house; it is now time to retire.

NORTH

The time from midnight to 3 A.M. is when the Sun is farthest away; it is the darkest part of the night, a time for secrets.

below A good night's sleep is essential for the maintenance of a healthy body.

Vastu Shastra also took into account natural factors, such as topography and climate, as well as dealing with the cultural needs of people. Rajasthan, in northern India, has a hot and desert-like climate so houses were built around a central courtyard onto which doors and windows opened. that would dissipate the excessive daytime heat by promoting air circulation The courtyard was also used as a place to socialize and to conduct various daily activities, such as sewing, knitting, and mixing spices. Stone was the normal building material, and the external walls were very thick so that the heat of the sun would not penetrate during the day. Instead, the walls absorbed the heat, releasing it during the much cooler night-time. This type of house was called a *haveli*, a name that possibly originates from the Hindi word for wind, *hava*.

On the other hand, Kerala in southern India has a wet and humid climate; here the houses had to cater for a very different environment. It was essential that the house design kept rooms damp-free. A house with three concentric squares around a central square courtyard was designed—humidity was managed by promoting the circulation of fresh air to each room. The outermost concentric square was a large open porch, the middle circle contained the living accommodation, and the inner square was another large open porch. The porches prevented the heavy monsoon rains from entering the house, and also encouraged good air circulation throughout the living area. Wood, plentiful in Kerala, was the main building material.

A house built along Vastu Shastra principles both supports, and helps its owner. A good design makes daily life easier and, if the owner maintains the contract between man and house, his home will be a holy space, providing blessings and protecting the occupants from harm, and promoting health, wealth, and harmony.

above *The exterior of the house must be well-maintained. A clean and well-tended garden and a well-lit entrance are all the harbingers of good, positive energies.*

above *Indian women tend to prepare and even cook their food in their courtyards. The women shown here are cleaning rice in their homes in Jaisalmer, Rajasthan.*

DIFFERENT MANDALAS USED IN VASTU SHASTRA

A mandala can contain any number of squares up to 1,024, provided that it always has a whole number as its square root. A typical mandala can have just one square or four squares, nine squares, and so on. The number of squares selected will depend on the size of the property or the type of building to be developed.

• A single square mandala is called a Sakala. It has four directions and is ruled by just four deities. Lord Kubera rules the north, Lord Yama the south, Lord Indra the east, and Lord Varuna the west. This type of mandala is used in the design of places dedicated to the worship of fire and ancestors.

• A mandala with four squares is called a Pechaka and is mainly used in the design of buildings for worship and public bathing.

• The Vastu Purusha Mandala with the nine-square grid is the one most frequently used. It is called the Pitha Mandala.

Each mandala has its own expanded representation of the eight primary directions. Irrespective of the number of squares in any mandala, the Purusha is usually lying face down, with his head in the northeast and his feet in the southwest. As the mandalas increase in complexity, they acquire further deities—although, in general, one deity is associated with each square, this is not a fixed rule and sometimes a deity has two or more squares. Even where a divinity is allotted more than one plot, the Lord Brahma—Creator of the Universe—always has the central one. Counting the squares should always start from the northeast, ruled by Lord Ishanna, and continue in a clockwise direction.

The *regents*, or main rulers, of the eight directions never change; they are Ishanna (god of purity) in the northeast, Indra (god of power) in the east, Agni (god of fire) in the southeast, Yama (god of justice) in the south, Niritti (god of misery) in the southwest,

Varuna (god of rain, oceans, rivers, and water) in the west, Vayu (god of wind) in the northwest, and Kubera (god of wealth) in the north. The additional gods, which are introduced as the mandala increases its number of squares beyond nine, will each possess attributes complementary to the main ruler of the direction into which the new deity is introduced.

left *North is ruled by the water element, south by earth, east by fire and west by air.*

VASTU PURUSHA MANDALA

Within each mandala, there is a correlation between the Purusha's body part and the function of the square in which it is placed. The purusha, for example, has his head in the northeast square; the head contains the brain and the mind, so the northeast room in the house is considered to be a proper place for worship. The house, as well as being the home of the Purusha, is also considered to be an extension of the owner.

A missing grid, plot or corner of the house means that the house is missing the luck of that corner for not just the owner of the house but for every member of the household. Since the VPM grid is square shaped and this is placed over a house when designing along Vastu Shastra principles it is important that you try to make the home square, or at least rectangular shaped.

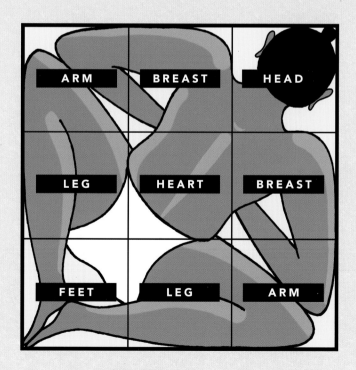

ARM	BREAST	HEAD
LEG	HEART	BREAST
FEET	LEG	ARM

left *It is believed that any flaw in any part of the house will bring an affliction to its owner, which will manifest itself in the part of his body corresponding to the Purusha's body part. For this reason, continuing maintenance of the house is vital for the owner's well-being.*

above *The Marble Pavilion and Bath House at Red Fort, India was built with Vastu Shastra principles in mind, with specific areas used according to the Vastu Purusha Mandala. Pictured here is the central courtyard, kept free of objects to honor the Lord Brahma.*

USING THE MANDALA

10
QUESTIONS
& ANSWERS

Q Does a Vastu Shastra consultant still work as part of a team of four people?

A Today's Vastu Shastra consultant generally works alone, establishing the overall parameters and helping to resolve difficult design conflicts. In the past, the team of four oversaw everything—from concept to completion—guiding the work of less skilful laborers. Nowadays architects, structural and civil engineers, and building designers carry out the concept and detailed design work, often under the supervision of a project manager.

Q I have read that the northeast sector is the "gateway to the gods." Is this true, and how do I maximize this area?

A The northeast sector is the source of positive cosmic energies. But an area for prayer does not have to be large—just take the northeastern wall, or corner, of your room, and place a picture or statue of your chosen god there. Or you could simply place a chair in that zone so that you can sit and meditate.

Q I live in an apartment in the city. Which room should I consider to be its center?

A The center is the part of the house where Lord Brahma resides—it can be either the center of the room in which you spend most of your time or the center of the house. Try to keep the center of your main living area clear of furniture and unnecessary clutter.

Q My house is only a couple of years old and doesn't appear to have had Vastu Shastra principles incorporated in its design. Can I still change it to follow Vastu guidelines?

A You can adapt the rooms in each sector in line with Vastu Shastra. Where you cannot change the function of a particular room, try to follow the Vastu guidelines as best you can. For example, if your bedroom doesn't lie in the most appropriate zone and you can't move it, then try moving your bed so that you have a beneficial sleeping direction.

Q I live in a house with a bathroom in the northeast sector. Where should I create my prayer area?

A Don't worry—just use the northeast corner, or side, of your living room or bedroom. Few people have a room that they can use solely for prayer and meditation. If you are still worried about this, you could move the bathroom, although it would prove very expensive.

Q Do I have to believe in all the nine deities present in the mandala and remember all their names and functions?

A You don't have to know any of the gods' names or functions to incorporate Vastu Shastra in your home. You can continue to follow your own religion—or believe in nothing— and still practice Vastu Shastra. The important thing is that the practical considerations are borne in mind.

Q My house is not square-shaped. Is it still possible to place the grid over it?

A While the preferred shape of a house is either square or rectangular, so that the mandala covers it perfectly, many houses are not built like this. If your house is irregular in shape, you can place the mandala over each individual room layout and work from there, getting the ideal function for each sector to fit within the different parts of the room.

Q If the nine-square mandala is the one most frequently used, does that mean that I have to have nine rooms in my house?

A You are partly right, in that the most commonly used mandala is the Vastu Purusha Mandala of nine squares. However, it can also be placed above a single room, thereby dividing the room into sectors. You can apply this principle to any house or apartment, irrespective of the number of rooms.

Q I am not a Hindu, but I would like to have "Om" displayed outside my main door. Is it alright to do that, or should I place it inside the house?

A You can display "Om" either inside or outside the house— just make sure that it is placed above the door and not on the floor, which is considerered disrespectful. Having the "Om" sign on your house is like having a talisman and is believed to bring blessings to the household.

Q Is it important to display pictures of the gods in each room, or on each wall, in order to receive their blessings?

A You don't need to display images of any of the gods unless you wish to. It is far more important that you follow your own personal beliefs while incorporating Vastu's practical guidelines.

4

A NEW
HOME

If you are looking for a new home, you might be one of those fortunate enough to be able to choose some land and build your own house. Often, though, we have to buy a previously owned house or a new house built by a developer. If you have the choice, and the finances, to find a plot and build from new, then take it. If you have to buy a pre-owned or pre-built property, then try to find one on a plot that gives you good Vastu Shastra attributes. Whatever you end up doing, you will almost certainly have to compromise on one or more features, but this chapter will help you to understand some of the attributes to look out for.

CHOOSING THE SITE FOR YOUR HOUSE

Having chosen the general part of the world where you want to live, the next thing to do is to select the plot or a property. Look for a plot in a neighborhood where the air is fresh and smells clean. The site should be free from any form of contamination, above or below ground. It should be a "green field" site, and not a previously used, or "brown field" site. It should be surrounded by similar land and not allocated for industrial or other similar development. It is important that you assess the area, both through official checks and by spending time there. If you cannot make the time yourself, try to get a friend or relative to help.

With regards to the building, although there might be a temptation to go for form instead of function, resist it. By all means go for style, but don't get caught out by fashion. The house you are looking for, or are going to build, will be

above *An area that supports the growth of vegetation, grass, and trees is recommended for siting a new house.*

above *In Vastu the shape of a house, the location, and which way the front door faces are all important considerations.*

your home; although its appearance is important, it should not be an end in itself. Decide on the type and size of building you want and choose a plot to accommodate it—a simple building is far better than a complex one and can also cost a lot less to build. You should try to get a regular shape; the closer it is to a square shape, the better. However, you may not be able to achieve this, and this chapter will show you ways of dealing with less-than-perfect plots.

SOIL ANALYSIS

In the practice of Vastra Shastra, it was believed that the land should possess one of 6 flavors; bitter, pungent, astringent, sweet, salty, or sour. The recommended color of the soil was white, red, or yellow. The soil had to be cool, pleasant, and smooth to the touch and should be free from bones, shells, ashes, gravel, sand, ants, and insects.

A test was carried out to assess the compactness of the soil. A pit was dug in the center of the site and the soil excavated and immediately put back, then inferences were drawn from the level of the replaced soil in the pit. The soil was considered inferior if the soil level fell below that of the pit, average if the soil filled to the rim of the pit, and superior if it overflowed the pit.

Another test was conducted to test the porosity of the soil. A pit was dug in the center of the site and then filled with water. The builder would then walk a hundred paces before returning to examine the level of the water in the pit. The soil was considered inferior if the water was completely absorbed, average quality if some of the water remained, and of superior quality if the water level remained unchanged.

The movement of the water was also tested. Still water indicated stability; counterclockwise movement indicated death; and clockwise indicated bliss.

The oxygen content of the soil was tested by placing an unbaked earthen lamp with four wicks in clarified butter in the pit. The soil was considered unsuitable if the lamp would not light. The suitability of the soil was also examined. In the pit were put four differently colored flowers. The suitability was tested by the ability of the flowers to withstand wilting or fading. The suitability of the soil was also examined by sowing an assortment of seeds. If the seed sprouted in 3 days, the soil was considered superior; if they sprouted after 5 days, it was of mediocre quality; and if they sprouted after 7 days the soil was considered to be inferior.

above *Decoration and the motifs used have an important part to play in the designing of a Vastu house.*

below *Plants need plenty of sunshine and water, and should be placed where they can get both.*

45

THE HISTORY

When you are close to making your choice, you should start looking at the history of the site or the building. Your realtor should be able to help you out with some of the information—but probably not as much as you will want to know. Sometimes, particularly with older properties, there is a limit on what you can find out—but do your best. The first contact point for information is, of course, the vendor. Also talk to the local council, neighbors, tradesmen, storeowners, and even the local library.

If you are looking for a pre-owned house, you should do your best to find one that has a happy history, or at least a neutral one. The history is indicative of the energies that prevail there. Within Vastu Shastra the belief is that the owner always has a close attachment to the house. If the owner is good to the house and looks after it, the house will be good to the owner in return and help him to become happier, more knowledgeable, and more successful. The owner will want to move from his home only for something better and more in keeping with his advancement through life's stages. You will want to buy a house that already has good happy energies to help you.

above *Every member of a family will benefit from a house that is built according to good Vastu principles.*

left *A well-tended garden and house attract positive energies, and can bring luck to all who live there.*

Sadly, some houses do have bad associations. We would not find good energies in a house that has associations with murder, violence, or sudden death. Perhaps during your enquiries you will learn that local folklore has tales of "strange goings-on" in years gone by; you will have to balance this with what the house has been like in the more recent past.

Treat bargain buys with caution; find out the reason for the low price. Maybe the vendor says that he wants a quick sale, but why? It might be because of some structural or geological fault, or it might be because the owner has gone bankrupt or the sale is forced because of an acrimonious divorce. Do you really want to buy that property with all the possible associated bad energies? Perhaps there are pressing reasons to say "yes" but weigh them up very carefully. Should you decide you want to purchase, then look for Vastu Shastra ways of negating any bad energy that might be present. Of course, it is equally possible that there is a very happy reason for the quick sale—perhaps the owner has got a good promotion and is moving to a different part of the country, or even another country. The house has been good to that owner!

below *All pieces of furniture must be cared for too, Vastu is about the whole environment not just the big things.*

right *An unkempt, neglected house does not attract good energies and so cannot promote health and success.*

THE PLOT OF LAND

Whether you are choosing a plot of land for a new building, or looking at an existing building on its plot, you will need to ask several questions. What is the shape? Is it regular or irregular? What is the topography or "lie of the land?" Is it flat or sloping? Who, or what, are the neighbors; there may be other houses nearby, or a school, hospital, or factory. Is the location a habitat for insect or animal life? What, if any, were its previous uses? Was it perhaps used as a sports field, a hospital, a factory or is it a landfill site? What is the obvious geology? Is it clay, sandy, rocky or barren? Is there a lake, a river, or another body of water close by? Prepare a checklist and, as you visit different properties, take notes and don't forget to record your overall impression. Unless you make notes, you will not be able to compare one site against the other later on.

A big plot of land does not necessarily mean there will be better Vastu Shastra. A small plot can have good Vastu Shastra—just make sure that you get value for money and stay within your budget. A one hundred percent perfect Vastu Shastra plot will not be easy to find—but just keep the essential Vastu shastra principles in mind and don't be overconcerned about the rest.

THE SHAPE

For residential properties, it is best to have a regular-shaped building, and the best regular shape to have is a square. Other shapes might be better for non-residential buildings; for instance round and oval shapes are considered ideal for sports or play activities. Although square is the optimum shape for the building itself, a slightly trapezoid shape is considered better for the plot. Where you have a trapezoid shape, the front should be narrower than the back. However, the world is not full of regular square-shaped plots. So, whatever plot you select, make sure that you have the potential to "create" a slightly trapezoidal square. You don't

right A square or rectangular extension in the northeast is considered to bring good luck in Vastu.

left Make a checklist of important things to look out for when buying a house.

have to change the property line or the fence. You can change the shape fairly simply by planting trees or shrubs—but do leave the northeast free. If the plot is L- or T-shaped, then perhaps you can divide it into two or three mini-plots, then consider each mini-plot individually. To do this, you place the mandala over each sub-plot and use the mandala to decide what its functions should be. Whatever the basic shape of the property, clever manipulation using greenery or the mandala, or both, can help you to optimize the energies that are present in the shape. In order to do this, you will have to consider the plot carefully and thoughtfully—be prepared to devote some time to its study.

THE TOPOGRAPHY

It is ideal for the plot to have a gentle slope running downward from the southwest to the northeast—this will bring peace, health, wealth, happiness, and harmony, and is the gateway to all that is good. Land with a slope toward the north, the east, or the west is also considered good. However, land that slopes to the south, southeast, southwest, and northwest is not so preferable—it is better to choose level land.

above *Good Vastu is ensured if you embark on a program of constant maintenance, both of your property and its environs.*

Avoid building on a plot with sides that slope downward toward the center, forming a depression. Also avoid a plot of land that forms a hillock, sloping from the center to the sides .

Whatever plot you choose, you must make sure that the slope can be accommodated in the overall design with respect to services and utilities, such as drainage, water supply, electricity, and piped gas. If in doubt, consult your architect or builder.

THE PLOT

It is suggested that, prior to building, all of these be graded accordingly.

• A plot that slopes toward the north is said to bring wealth and happiness.

• A plot that slopes toward the east is said to bring success and well-being.

• A plot that slopes toward the west is said to bring knowledge and wealth.

THE NEIGHBORS

Take a careful look at who, or what, your neighbors are. Perhaps there are no neighbors—yet! If that is the case, then check whether or not any sort of development has been planned for the area—commercial, industrial, or residential—and don't forget to check out for future roads. See if there are any legal covenants that can protect you from unwelcome developments in the future.

Some neighborhoods just do not dispense very positive energies—you can see it straightaway. Neighborhoods that do not emanate auspicious or positive energies might incorporate a casino or other gambling place, a bar or club, a hospital, or a place for spent or used goods—such as a landfill site, or a cemetery or other place of the dead. You should avoid moving into these areas if you can. There are other areas, such as those with parks, lakes, rivers, or well-tended buildings, which give out good energies and they are the ones that you should consider.

It is always good to have natural sunlight washing all over your plot for as much of the day as possible. Try to avoid plots where large buildings, or structures, overshadow your property. Any adjacent property should be considered in relation to the plot or building that you are hoping to purchase or rent. Adjacent buildings should be an adequate distance away from your property. It is difficult to define what "adequate" is, because it will depend so much on the size of the house you might want to buy or build. It will come down to judgement; if in doubt, ask a couple of friends.

Your house should not be dwarfed by the buildings next to it—avoid constructing, or buying, a house between two tall buildings, which would overpower it. Of course, if you buy a row or town house you won't have to deal with that particular issue. But make sure you choose a town house that is radiated by the sun's

above *A house that has an attractive view, especially over a body of water or a well-kept garden, will always be coveted.*

beneficial rays. A small open space in front of the house is a plus, as this will attract positive energies and let them collect and pool before meandering inside and around the house.

As with so many things in life, you might have to compromise. If, for personal, financial, or business reasons, you have to live in the middle of a large city, such as London, New York, or Paris, you will have to recognize that you won't be able to change too much of what is there—but you will at least know what you should be looking for.

THE LOCATION

Rocky or barren terrain is considered to be very poor ground for building residences—unless, of course, you live in a desert location and you have no alternative. It is preferable to choose land with sweet, fresh soil that has not been previously used for industrial, waste disposal, military, or defense purposes. If this is the case, then it must be thoroughly decontaminated before further use. It is also advisable to ensure there are no problems with natural infestations, ranging from wasps to rats, locusts, and rattlesnakes.

If you are able to purchase a property overlooking a body of water, such as a lake or river, it can be very good. Living near water will bring very auspicious energies into your home, but take care that you don't choose a flood plain on which to build your house. For a Vastu Shastra design, it is best when the body of water is to the north of the property. The water should be clean and flowing—in the case of a lake or pond, it should not be stagnant. It should not have effluent deposited into it and should be capable of sustaining life and providing food for fishes and birds. It is better to avoid locations where the sound of water constantly and excessively assaults the ears. Gently moving water is soothing to the ears and nerves and attracts positive beneficial energies. If there is no natural body of water present, then building artificial features—ponds, fountains, streams—can bring positive energies to a property.

In particular, water attracts energies that can lead to prosperity. There are many examples of prosperous cities built overlooking water—Hong Kong, Singapore, San Francisco, Los Angeles, Vancouver, Sydney, and London. Use the power of water to help you.

above *Ganesha, the elephant god, is worshipped at the beginning of every important step, such as moving house.*

right *A house that faces water, such as this mountain lake, is ideal in Vastu Shastra, since it is believed to enhance prosperity.*

VASTU SHASTRA CONSIDERATIONS
FOR WEALTH AND WELL-BEING

When you are looking for a plot or property, it is quite likely that
you will want to choose one that will help you to become richer,
whether in mind, body, spirit, or more material things. In Vastu
Purusha Mandala, the deities that rule the north, east, and
northeast represent all life's positive processes. The balanced and
cool areas of the north zones have positive energies with good,
divine, and auspicious effects that can bring material happiness,
bliss, and contentment of the five senses—sight, hearing, smell,
taste, and touch. New beginnings and important decisions should
be made and taken when facing, or present in, the north direction.
All houses with openings such as walls or doors in the north or east
are considered "heavenly abodes." Creative work and promotional
activities should take place here. Try to leave as much open space
as is possible and practical in the north and east; the more there is,
the better it is for energies and luck. Having open space here
exposes household members to the health-preserving energies of
the morning sun.

The energies in the south and southwest, on the other hand,
are considered to be disturbed and are supposed to represent "the
curse of nature." In Vastu Purusha Mandala, destructive deities, all
with negative energies, rule the south, southwest, and west
directions. Try to avoid being in, or facing, these directions when
making important decisions or new beginnings.

right *Lord Brahma
dwells in the center
of the house, and it is
considered essential
to keep this area
empty and free.*

KEY

Positive area

Negative area

Moderate area

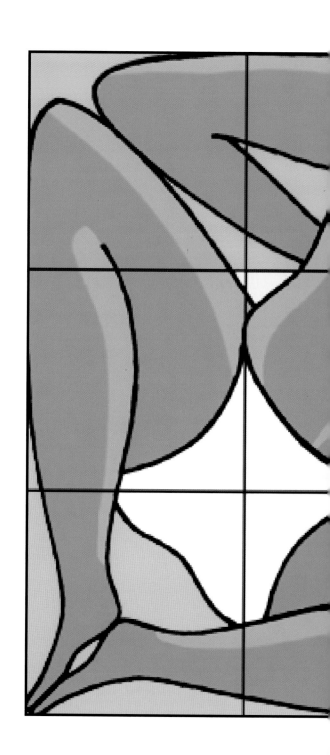

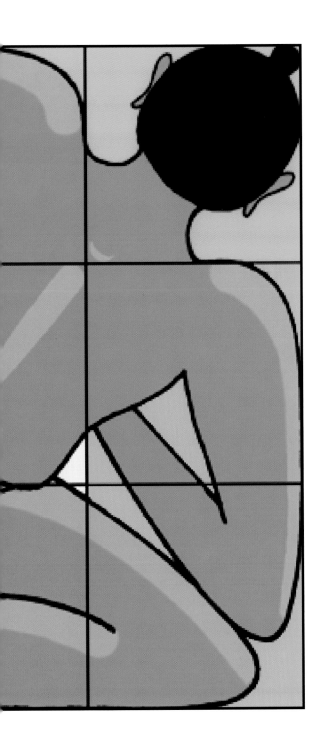

THE RECOMMENDATIONS IN VASTU SHASTRA ARE:

- Try to avoid having too many openings facing south or west.
- Plant trees in the southern areas.
- Try to avoid having trees in the north, east, or northeast zones.
- Generally, boundary walls in the south and southwest should be higher and thicker than elsewhere.
- Terraces should be in the north, east, and northeast zones of the property.
- In multistorey buildings, which do not have a uniform number of floors, there should be more floors in the southwest sector than in the northeast.
- Use landscaping as a means of elevating south and southwest zones.
- Roofs and ground that slope from the southern and western zones toward the northern and eastern zones are preferred.
- A slope toward the southwest is not recommended.
- A slope toward the center of the property is not recommended.
- Land that is elevated in the northeast, east, and southeast is not preferred.
- Triangular, circular, and irregular shapes are inferior for residential use; they are believed to lead to instability.
- A plot with an extended northeast direction is considered to be auspicious.
- A plot with an extension in the southwest is believed to present a potential risk to its owners.

A NEW HOME

10
QUESTIONS
& ANSWERS

Q I have been left a plot of land and want to build a new house on it. I would like to use Vastu Shastra principles, but it is an L-shaped plot. What should I do?

A You could separate the property into two plots and build on one. Alternatively, you could build a house by overlaying the mandala on each "leg" of the "L"-shape. The important rule in Vastu Shastra is that the preferred shape of the property is square or rectangular, and you would have met this requirement.

Q My dining area is in the southwest and on the same level as the rest of the house. How could I set about elevating it, as recommended by Vastu principles?

A It depends on the height of your rooms. If you live in an old house, you may have very high ceilings, and could make a feature using an elevated platform. Don't forget safety—you might need to add a balustrade around the edge. On the other hand, if the ceiling is low, then you could build a platform just three or four inches high. Be careful about the potential tripping hazard that this might create.

Q I have a terrific house, but there is no slope at all in the garden. How can I create one, in line with Vastu guidelines?

A You have a choice: either leave it as it is, or use soil to create a small raised garden in the southwest, with a slight slope running downhill to the northeast (from where the soil has been removed). The sloping section doesn't have to be a large area or very high. You can either make a feature of it or blend it in to fit the feel of the planting so that it is barely noticeable.

Q I have recently moved house and now live very close to a high school. Is that good or bad, according to Vastu?

A Schools, playgrounds, parks, and gardens all have positive energies. They are lively, exuberant, happy places, which naturally attract positive energies and keep negative energies at bay. Attraction of such positive energies to your home or property is vital in Vastu Shastra. It is therefore beneficial to live in such areas—but be prepared for the boisterousness of young people!

Q I have a large garden and want to build a rock feature with a small fountain. Where should I position it?

A The earth element belongs to the southwest and water to the north. A feature in the north, east, or northeast must be smaller than one in the south, west, or southwest (the water in a fountain being included in its size). If water is in a fixed location—not flowing from one direction to another—then it should be in the north. It is alright to have a rockery here, as long as the "rocks" are not too large.

Q I live in a square-shaped apartment with an outside terrace with a curved balustrade. What can I do to make it more regular in shape?

A There are a couple of options, but your choice will be dictated by the size of your terrace. You could either put suitable pot plants in front of the balustrade to create a straight line, or you could build some simple seating, which is curved at the back and straight at the front.

Q I work in an office with ten other people. We are all interested in Vastu Shastra and wonder where we should place a decorative water feature?

A The element of water rules the north sector of a property, so it is good to have water in this area. If you have a kitchen in the north sector of the office, you can put your water feature there. A water dispenser or cooler in the north part of the kitchen would also fulfill Vastu Shastra principles and would be functional, too.

Q I have seen a plot of land on which I would like to build a house. It was private parkland before being sold off for residential development. Should I carry out soil tests to see if the land is good?

A Since it was a garden, the land is probably good. Dry, barren land is not recommended for building on, but land that supports life—either plant or animal—is sought-after. If the plot was private parkland and rich in plants and flowers, then you shouldn't need to do any soil tests—at least not from a Vastu Shastra standpoint.

Q I have always lived in apartments and now I want to buy a house in the city. Does it matter which way the house faces?

A If you wish to follow Vastu Shastra principles. it is recommended that you buy a house that faces east, north, or northeast, since these are the directions associated with more positive energies and they will enhance your good luck. The least sought-after properties, according to Vastu Shastra, are those that face south, west, and southwest.

Q I am looking for a new house and have seen two that I like. The lower-priced one is next to a vacant site on which either industrial or residential development is planned. Which house would be best, according to Vastu Shastru guidelines?

A The lower price possibly reflects the uncertainty of the future development. If the new building turns out to be residential, then that would be the house to choose; if it turns out to be industrial, then it could be almost any kind of factory and may not be so beneficial to you.

5
STRUCTURAL
FEATURES

In this chapter, we will look at some of the more general "structural" items in a house. What do we do about water, which will be used extensively inside the house? What is the best location for the main door—what do we have to consider and what must we avoid? Where should the staircase be installed in a multistorey home? Where should the garage be? What should a basement be used for?

WATER FOUNTAIN

THE IMPORTANCE OF WATER STORAGE AND DISPOSAL

In Vastu Shastra, water is one of the five important elements. It is believed to bring prosperity and wealth and is cleansing, life-preserving, and life-enhancing. A home must have an adequate supply of water for washing, bathing, laundry, and cleaning. The presence of water in close vicinity to a home is also very beneficial. If you have a home that is close to flowing water or, better still, overlooking it, then you are very fortunate, but generally these ideal locations have far from ideal prices. If you have neither the fortune nor good luck to live near a natural body of water, then you can still benefit from water by building an artificial water feature to attract the positive energies.

WATER CYLINDER

An artificial water feature can be anything from a large fountain, lake, or pond to a very small glass cylinder filled with water with a pump to keep it bubbling away. Your choice will depend on the size of your property, your preference, and, of course, your budget. If you can manage to have a feature, then do so; according to Vastu Shastra, this can bring only good luck. The main rule for water is that it must be clean and must never be left to stagnate.

The water element is associated with the north direction, which is ruled by Kubera, the god of wealth. To take full advantage of the wealth connection, you should try to have your water feature,

BAMBOO
WATER FEATURE

above Artificial water features can be used to attract wealth and bring good luck. They can be placed either inside the house or outside in the garden.

POT WATER FEATURE

STONE WATER
FEATURE

SMALL STREAM

far right *A south-facing bathroom will be bathed in sunlight as it streams through the window. The heat of the sun will keep the room clean and dry.*

whether natural or artificial or both, in the northern part of your house. In a northeast-facing house—that is, a house where the entrance faces northeast—you should place any external artificial water feature close to the entrance, but in the northern sector. Try to keep the northeast part of the property as open and uncluttered as possible—this will let the energies enter the house, and flow through it easily.

Your house will have several "wet" areas; the place where your water tank is, the kitchen, and one or more bathrooms. You may also have a utility room for your washing machine and drier.

WATER STORAGE

During the construction phase of a home, the water supply should be brought into the north, east, or northeast sector. It is worth noting that, even during construction, those parts should not be used as a general storage area, they should be used solely as a water supply area—whether piped in or brought in by tanker. Water for the house can be stored in the roof space or below ground. During the design phase, it is suggested that any overhead tank should be placed in the southwest or south side or sector. If you choose to have an underground tank, from which the water will be pumped through the house, then locate it in the north, east, or even in the northeast zone. Used water (in other words, unclean water) should be suitably disposed of, in any direction except the northeast.

THE KITCHEN

The southeast sector is the recommended area for the kitchen since fire rules this sector. Since water is used extensively in the kitchen, it is suggested that the sink, dishwasher, and washing machines are best located in the north. Any water cooler or dispenser, or even an ice-making machine, should, where possible, be put in this sector. If they cannot fit there for any reason, then use another sector, but remember not to place them in the northeast or in the center of the room. The kitchen should be close to the dining room, but not next to a bathroom or to the main entrance of the house.

above *The kitchen should ideally be located in the southeast sector of the house.*

THE BATHROOMS

Bathrooms, like kitchens, should never be located in either the northeast sector of the house, or the center of the house. Vastu Shastra recommends that they be located in the south sector where they will get the maximum effect of the sun in "drying them out," thereby keeping the house hygienically clean and dry. It is best to locate the shower or washbasin in the north or east sector of the bathroom, while the water closet and bidet is best in the west, south, or northwest sector. The bathtub, the heaviest item when full, should be placed in the southern area. Within a small bathroom—bearing in mind that there will also have to be room to open the door—some compromise will almost certainly be necessary when locating the various fittings. But this is fine—the arrangement of rooms and fittings don't have to be perfect to benefit from Vastu Shastra.

above *It is important to ensure that the door of the bathroom is not located directly opposite the main door of the house.*

above *Vastu Shastra recommends that the main front door should be made of strong, solid wood and should also be the biggest door in the house.*

BEST LOCATIONS FOR STAIRCASES

On any staircase there should always be an odd number of steps. A staircase should not be in the center of the house, as this is where Lord Brahma resides, and if possible and practical it should be located anywhere other than the northeast sector or center of the house. The underside of a staircase should not be inside another room. It can be "boxed in" for use as a storage area, for bookshelves, or it can even be used to incorporate a shower or bathroom, but it should not form part of a ceiling of another room. Where choice is available, staircases are best located in the southwest, south, or west sections of the house. The staircase should rise from east to west or from north to south. The center of the house is where the Lord Brahma resides and you should keep it free, open, and well-lit.

BEST LOCATIONS FOR DOORS AND WINDOWS

Any opening to the property, whether a door or window, is important because it determines what energy comes into your house. Special care must be given to the main door of the house.

The main door should be the biggest door in the house, and more elaborate, but in proportion to the size of the home. It should be well painted and kept clean. The door should be strong and preferably made from wood. Ideally, the main door is located at the front of the house, facing toward a road.

According to Vastu Shastra, any door that is in the northeast, north, or east of the property is good as it lets the positive cosmic energy come into the house. A door should not be located at the precise center of a cardinal direction—at 90°, 180°, 270°, or 360° of the compass; it should always be a little to the side of to those points. Leave some open space in front of the door, both inside and outside, so that the energies can gather here before they circulate around the rooms. Energy should not stagnate in any corner and no cumbersome furniture be placed around the door or passages that lead to, or from, it. Keep all the doors in the house clutter-free so that they can open all the way, and try not to use the backs of the doors for anything. Ensure that your main door is not in a direct line with any objects that are considered harmful.

Any driveway or path that leads to the main door should be curving to let positive energy meander into the house. In India, people decorate their front door quite elaborately, adorning them with an image of a god or decorating them with fresh flowers. This is done to discourage any evil energy from entering the house.

above The ideal use for a basement is as an exercise room or a children's play area.

Houses that face north, east, and northeast will receive the best of the sunlight heralding positive energy into the house. Windows and doors are greatly recommended here. An open area in the northeast, such as a terrace, is considered beneficial. If your windows face these directions, open them often so that the property benefits from positive energy.

The south, west, and southwest parts of your house should have few openings because the sun is too strong here and is not positive. You should keep the windows and doors in this sector closed as much as possible. You should also avoid having windows on more than two walls in any one room.

above A window that is in direct line with a tree is not good vastu; a screen or fence could be used to shield the offending site.

BEST LOCATIONS OF STOREROOMS, GARAGES, BASEMENTS, AND CELLARS

If you live in a house that has storerooms, garages, and basements or cellars, you should use them for storage, or for exercise or other recreational purposes. These rooms are not recommended for conducting any form of business or for studying.

Storerooms should be located in the south, southwest, or west, of a house. Within the storeroom, place the heaviest items in the southwest, west, or south sectors. If you have a storeroom in the north, east, or northeast part of the house, try to have more windows in this section so that the positive energies can enter here. You can also encourage positive energies by ensuring you have the minimum amount of clutter.

above Any objects that are not needed, or used, should be stacked away in boxes, or given to friends, relatives, or charities.

GARAGES

The best places for the garage are in the northwest, southeast, or southwest part of the house or property. It should not be in the northeast section of your house. A garage separated from the main house is far preferred to one that is attached.

CELLARS/BASEMENTS

These rooms are not really recommended for accommodation since daylight will rarely penetrate to rooms that are located beneath ground level. If you have no alternative but to live in such a place, then make every endeavor to give yourself as much artificial light as possible. The entrance to a basement or cellar should be in the north, east, or northeast section of the property.

Basements are best used for car parks, for mechanical equipment, and for the storage of goods, old records, and so on. Once again, the south, southwest, and the west part of the basement are best suited for the storage of heavier items, while the northeast, east, and north part of the cellar or basement should be as sparsely filled as is possible and practical.

The southwest, west, and south section of the basement and cellar should be left as quiet as possible and any doors here should be kept shut whenever not in use. There is always a great temptation to fill garages and basements with things that are out of date, or that you consider might come in useful some time in the future. Avoid the temptation—get rid of clutter.

above *A garage should be built slightly away from the main house, and should ideally be located in the northwest sector of the plot.*

far right *Regular spring cleaning is essential to get rid of unwanted things and to keep the house clutter-free.*

STRUCTURAL FEATURES

10

QUESTIONS
& ANSWERS

Q What can I do about my driveway to make it more Vastu-friendly? It runs in a straight line from my gate to my main door and is about 60 feet long.

A You could either move your gate and have a gentle curve laid toward the door, or leave the gate where it is and move the drive so that it curves toward the door—perhaps placing plants alongside it to enhance the curve.

Q We have a basement in our house, which is approached by two external staircases and which has two doors, one at the front of the house (east) and the other at the back (west). Which door should we use?

A Try to keep the door in the west closed and locked as much as possible, because this is not the most auspicious direction for a doorway to face. Use the door in the east, as this direction allows positive cosmic energy to enter your home.

Q I have an even number of steps in my staircase. Would an odd number be more acceptable, according to Vastu guidelines?

A Yes, although it is not going to be easy to alter the number of stairs unless you are prepared to change the whole staircase, which could be very expensive. You could try adding a small riser to the bottom step, although this might become a safety hazard. If you really want to change your staircase, I suggest that you talk to an architect.

Q I have a garage attached to my house, with a bedroom above it, in the northeast sector. What can I do to bring this into line with Vastu principles?

A The northeast is where the auspicious energies are, but a garage and bedroom are not the best rooms to have located here. If you can park your car elsewhere, then do so; if you have another bedroom in the house, use that instead. You can continue to use the bedroom above the garage, but keep its northeast sector lightly furnished and free of heavy furniture.

Q The front door of my house is located in the southwest sector of the overall plan. Is it all right to use it?

A If you have a back door in, say, the northeast sector, that would be a better choice. However, if you have to use the front door, don't worry about it—we have to live our lives and compromise at times.

Q I live in a studio apartment and plan to get a small indoor water feature. Where is the best place to put this?

A Water, according to Vastu Shastra, is believed to enhance wealth. The north sector is ruled by this element, so the best location for your water feature is the north section or wall of the apartment. Please ensure that the water always flows freely and that the water feature is cleaned periodically to keep dirt and dust away.

Q I am designing a house along Vastu Shastra principles and would like to know whether a spiral staircase is acceptable?

A Vastu Shastra recommends having "square-shaped" staircases that climb in line and, where necessary, turn at right angles. This is because the square shape belongs to the earth element and has a quiet energy, which is more sought-after in homes and offices. The circle or spiral shape belongs to the water element and is believed to promote active and aggressive energy. This shape should be used only when you want to cultivate these types of energy.

Q I have a water feature under the staircase. Is that good Vastu Shastra?

A Having a water feature is fine in itself, since water is associated with enhancing wealth. Water in the north sector of the house is preferable, because this sector is ruled by the water element. If your staircase is in the north sector of your house, then a water feature would be most appropriate here. Water should not be positioned in the southwest, west, or south sectors or center of the house.

Q My father uses our garage as his personal storeroom and our family car no longer fits in it. What should we do about all his papers and clutter?

A Clutter blocks the flow of energy and should be cleared away. If your father needs all the space and his papers are important to him, then he need not get rid of them—just help him store them neatly in boxes, then place them in the southwest section of his study. The southwest area should have heavy objects to suppress the negative energy that originates there.

Q I live in an apartment building and we have a lift in the middle of the building. Is that bad Vastu Shastra?

A There are only certain things over which you have any control —so just consider your apartment and ignore the rest of the building. Very few buildings in the west have been built according to Vastu Shastra principles. Your focus should be on your own apartment and its interior layout.

6

MAKING CORRECTIONS

Most of us live in homes that have been built without any knowledge of Vastu Shastra principles, and the building may, therefore, be in conflict with the aims of Vastu Shastra. If that is the case, what can be done? Very few of us could possibly afford to knock down and rebuild our homes, and that wouldn't even be an option for apartment-dwellers. It is possible, however, to assess your home from a Vastu Shastra viewpoint and see what is feasible. If you happen to live in an apartment, you are far more limited, but you can concentrate on controlling or readjusting your apartment inside and not concern yourself with the rest of the building.

Let us start by looking at the inside of the house or apartment, beginning with the main entrance. A solid wooden door is recommended for the main entrance, and it should be larger than any of the other doors within the home. The area immediately behind the door should be free of any clutter, and there should be no furniture immediately behind or near the door, enabling it to open all the way without any hindrance. The door should open without squeaking or creaking—the hinges should be smooth and quiet. The door should be clean, and dust- and dirt-free, and there should be nothing hanging on the back of the door. The area near the main door should be well lit and welcoming. All of these considerations are easily taken care of, with the help of paint, oil, and elbow grease!

There should not be a wall immediately in front of the main door; if that is the case, you can counteract its negative impact by placing some welcoming feature on it. An example of a welcoming feature might be a tapestry, a plant, an uplighter, a photograph, a

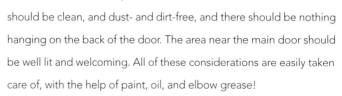

above *The seating in this living room is well laid-out, leaving the center of the room unobstructed.*

picture, a curio, or a picture of an idol of any god that you believe in. If the door is in the north sector of the house, you can have a blue-colored tapestry on the wall. If you have a longish passage in front of the main door, opening onto various rooms, try to keep this area well lit and make sure it is brightly decorated. Since energy speeds up when it travels in a straight line, it helps if any long passage has some means of slowing the energy down— think of placing extra lights, pictures, or plants there.

It is believed that the god Lord Brahma resides in the center of the house and hence this area of the property should be kept both open and well lit. If you live in a small apartment or a house that doesn't have an open center, focus instead on the center of each of the individual rooms and try, as far as possible, to leave the centers free of furniture. If you have any rooms that are not square or rectangular in shape, which are considered the optimum shapes in Vastu Shastra, then you can arrange your furniture in a way that creates a partition in order to create square spaces within the rooms. This can be done using, say, a bookshelf, cabinet, screen, or dividers. The single room then becomes two different rectangular or square-shaped spaces.

above *Plants can be used to great effect when bringing your home in line with Vastu principles.*

below *This long passage is well lit and pleasingly decorated, enhancing and encouraging the flow of energy to the rest of the house.*

above *Color can be introduced in lamps, blinds, cushions, walls, and sofas to enhance an energy or element.*

It is not considered very auspicious to paint the entire interior of the house white. But, if this is the case, you don't have to repaint any of the house, you can just alleviate the all-pervading white with the use of colors in throws, rugs, carpets, cushions, curtains, and so on.

One of the key attributes of a Vastu Shastra home is that it is clean and clutter-free. Keeping your home clean is a natural priority, but eliminating clutter can be very hard indeed. It will, however, go a long way toward improving the energies of your home. Look at all your possessions—clothes, soft furnishings, electrical equipment, furniture, books, and magazines. Ask yourself if you really need them all. When was the last time you wore, read, or used them? Are you clinging to possessions simply because you have had them for a long time? Do you really need to keep them? Is there a school, children's home, old folks' home, or charity organization that can put your excess belongings to immediate use? When you have asked and answered all of these questions honestly, you might find that you can actually get rid of some clutter. And if no one wants it, then see if it can be recycled in some way before you throw it away.

right *Throw rugs, tapestries, and carpets can also be used to soften harsh edges, plain walls, and corners.*

Have a look at your northeast areas—remember that, in Vastu Shastra, this area is "the gateway to the gods." It should be comparatively open and lightly furnished. If, on the other hand, you have a kitchen or a bathroom in the northeast, what can you do about it? Much will depend on your finances—moving electrical and plumbed equipment is not cheap. It might be more pragmatic to assess what can be done to mitigate the situation. If the stove is not in the best position within the kitchen, you could perhaps maximize the use of portable cooking equipment, such as a portable electric stove or a microwave, rice cooker, or toaster, which could be located in a more favorable area. If you cannot relocate the sink, then you could resolve instead not to leave water standing in it for any length of time, keep the waste pipe as clean as possible and always flushed well with clean water, and ensure that water-containing vessels are spotlessly clean. The same principles apply to the bathroom, which should also be kept spotlessly clean.

above *It is a good idea to place any electrical equipment, such as toasters, kettles, or microwaves, in the southeast section of the kitchen, which is ruled by fire.*

right *A bathroom in the eastern sector of the house is ideal, since it will receive maximum sunlight, keeping the place clean and dry.*

OUTSIDE THE HOUSE

Many new buildings quickly look as if they have been standing for decades—tired and run down. A house has to be well maintained, and that means fixing the roof and gutters, keeping the drains clean, painting the building, cleaning up the garden, cutting the grass, trimming the hedges. Just keeping a house clean and well-tended can make a miraculous difference. Your home should always be a joy to look at—it should fit in amongst the other buildings and should look like it "belongs." Even if the exterior of your house is painted white, you can add colour to the windows, gates, doors, fences, and so on, to relieve the starkness.

Make sure that the outside of the house or the property is well lit and the number or name of the property is easy to read. The main entrance to the property should always look well-lit, clean, and welcoming. Thorny plants should not be grown near the entrance to your property. Sometimes these plants are used to deter burglars—if this is the case, look for other ways to keep them out, and get rid of the thorny plants.

There should never be any garbage outside the house or any stagnant water near the main entrance. Keep your garbage in a well-sealed bin, and preferably in a bin store. The entrance to your house or property should be higher than that of the main outside road. If it isn't, then you will probably have to accept it, and look for better next time. The staircase or the driveway that leads to your

house should not be broken, damaged, or falling apart or in a general state of disrepair—if it is, then make sure you repair it. The main door to the house should always open inward; if it opens outward you should find out why and if there is no good reason, change it to open inward.

Ideally, there should be no electric poles, posts, or pylons close to your house. If your front main door is in direct line with a pillar, a lamp post, a tree, or a road that points straight toward it, then this is considered to be an "arrow" which is believed to have harmful potential for the people who live in the house. The best way to escape this harmful effect is to build a hedge of some sort, or to construct a fence that will at least deflect some of the bad or negative energies. If there is a gate in line between the door and the post, see if you can move the gate.

If there are trees or a high wall in the northeast, north, or east section of your property, raise the level of the property on the opposite side by raising the level of an existing fence, or planting tall trees to lower the north, east, and northeast section. You will then invite positive energy in and keep out the negative.

Pay attention to your property. You can clean, wipe, dust, paint, trim, cut, rearrange, and renew, and thereby let new energies into your home.

right *Thorn-bearing plants are believed to chase away good energies and are therefore not recommended near the main entrance.*

SPEARING ROAD

A road that runs directly towards the front facing of a plot is called a "spearing" road and a house that protrudes on to a road is said to be "speared" by the road. Below are examples of "good" and "bad" spearings. Bad spearings are not auspicious and should be avoided.

Above is an example of a road that runs into the front of the house—this house is "speared" by the road. The house faces south and is considered "bad" Vastu.

A house that faces west and where the southwest, west, and northwest parts of the plot are speared by the road is not auspicious.

A house that faces northeast when the east, northeast, and north parts of the plot of the house are speared by the road is an auspicious house.

A house that faces southwest and where the south, southwest, and west plot of the house is speared by the road is not an auspicious house.

A house that faces north with the northwest, north, and northeast sections of the plot speared by the road is not an auspicious house.

A house that faces east with the southeast, east, and northeast parts of the plot being speared by the road is an auspicious house.

HANDLING MISSING CORNERS
AND IRREGULARLY SHAPED PLOTS

The reason that Vastu Shastra considers a square shape to be the best for buildings and plots of land is that the square shape belongs to the earth element, which is considered good for residential buildings and plots. Not all of us live in a regular-shaped property, however, and uneven or irregular-shaped properties, no matter how interesting, do present problems when it comes to Vastu Shastra, since "missing" corners or sections may lead to missing energies. In these circumstances, it is recommended that you "change" the shape of your property so that you eliminate any missing corners.

Outside the house, the plot of land can be squared off by building a fence, growing hedges, or even using garden furniture to create partitions. When it comes to the shape of the building itself it may even be possible—but expensive—to add a wing to your house, thereby squaring it off. Far less expensive would be to "build" a partition, which can be used to divide the exterior plot. If the shape of the property is T-shaped, for example, you can use partitions to create two plots, and use one section for the house construction, and the other section for the garden. If the shape of the house is trapezoid, plant trees in such a way that you create a square shape.

above Strategically placed plants can be used to "square off" irregularly-shaped areas.

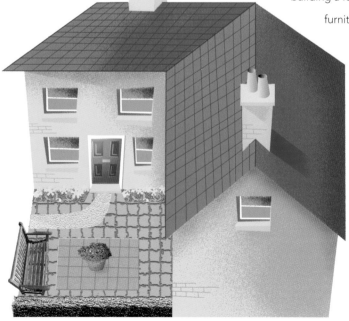

below The missing sectors and corners of this L-shaped house have been rectified by the design of the patio, which creates a square-shaped plot.

If you have the space and want to build an extension, then build in the northeast, north, or east section of the house. This is considered very auspicious since this section, being the gateway to the gods, is the source of all positive cosmic energies. But take care that any extension you build is a square or rectangular shape. An extension in the southwest, south, or west of the house is not considered auspicious.

Amazingly, houses that are narrow in the front and broader at the back (a shape called a *gaumukh*), are, despite being irregular, considered auspicious since they are believed to be in the shape of a cow's face, and in India the cow is considered to be a "holy" animal. However, a plot that is broad at the front and narrow at the back, known as the *vaghmukh* shape, is considered inauspicious since it is shaped like the face of a tiger. If you have a *vaghmukh*-shaped house, try and use the broader, front side of the house as much as possible for doing most of the important work and use the back narrow portion of the house as a playroom, hobby room, tool room, or as a utility room or pantry. When it comes to individual rooms, you might be able to square up any irregular shapes by building closets, bookshelves, and so on.

below *Children's toys need to be cared for according to Vastu. Their choice is up to you but they should be kept tidy and if broken they should be fixed.*

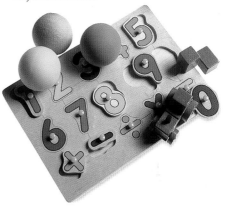

below right *An L-shaped house has missing sectors and corners and therefore missing energies and luck. This can be rectified by building an extension to create a regular square shape.*

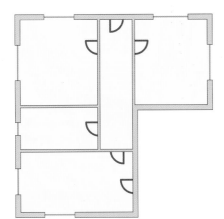

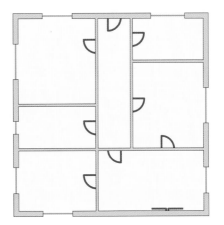

left *The square shape belongs to the earth element and is considered ideal for living, hence the perfect Vastu Shastra house is square or rectangular in shape.*

above *Toys should not be left strewn around after play—they should be stacked and stored away in a designated box or cupboard.*

CREATING A FAMILY HOME

Your house or apartment should meet the needs of every member of the household—from the owner to the youngest child. You should have sufficient rooms to ensure that each family member has his or her space, and each room is designed to serve its function. This does not mean that each child must have his or her own bedroom; but each should have his or her own bed and storage area. You can store the toys and books that the children collect in their bedroom or you can create a "play corner" within the room, which they can use whenever they want. Toys and books must be stored away neatly in a cupboard; toy boxes should be kept neatly stacked. If you have a basement, you can make a playroom there, where the children can keep their toys and games. This will also be a special place where they can go when their friends come over to play. If the adults have hobbies, they might need space for storing their equipment and tools—basements or garages are ideal for that purpose.

The important family rooms are the dining room and the living room where the family members get together to eat, talk about the day's events, family matters, read with the children, or even watch television or listen to music together. These rooms should be large enough, with sufficient seating, to ensure that all the family members can gather and sit comfortably facing toward each other.

Fill the living room with objects that are meaningful to the family—photographs and mementos of joyous occasions.

left *Dining in a well-lit, well laid out, and tidy room can make eating a more enjoyable event for the whole family.*

THE "HEALING" HOME

Do you yearn to get back home after a long day at work? When your home has restful, peaceful energies and you feel comfortable and at ease there, then you are on the road to living in harmony with the environment. Do you, on the other hand, spend as much time as possible away from home and find yourself waking up exhausted and tired even after an early night? If this is what is happening to you, perhaps you would benefit from taking a careful and closer look both at your work and home environments.

Just as there are hyperactive people in the world, there are also "active" restless energies around us, and we have to think carefully about which type of energy we want to access. Do you work in a loud, bright active office and yearn for calmer, peaceful, and restful energies? Or is it the other way around, and you find yourself hankering after brighter, more cheerful, louder energies?

below A bedroom that promotes restful, calm, and relaxing energies is important for a good night's sleep.

above The effects of creating a "healing" home can be felt throughout your daily life—even in the office.

Whatever the place that you are designing or planning, you have to make the best use of space for the benefit of the entire household. In India, traditional houses or buildings were constructed around a central courtyard, known as the *bindu*. It was from here that positive energy radiated to the rest of the rooms in the house. This center was free of any clutter or furniture and devoid of any "functional" rooms.

The size of the central area was dependent on the size of the house—the bigger the house, the bigger the area. This open space protected the members of the house from the harsh, hot winds blowing outside; it was also a private section of the house where family members could get together to gossip and interact. The holy plant, called *tulsi*, believed to purify the air and known for its medicinal value, was planted in this part of the house. The center of the house represented inner consciousness and space. Any damage to the center was thought to lead to difficulties for the members of the house.

above *Creating a Vastu Shastra environment at home can help protect you from the stresses outside, keeping you safe within.*

If you have an identifiable center in your house, then try to emulate the traditional Indian household by keeping it free of furniture. If you do not have a central area, then take the center of each room and keep that as empty as possible.

It is considered that the north, northeast, and east are the directions from which the positive, beneficial energies come. The northeast section of your home should be open and spacious, or alternatively it should have as many windows as are possible and practical. Since positive energy flows from the northeast to the southwest, it is advisable to let it spread and meander all over the house—encourage energy to flow by ensuring that the northeast is free of clutter

below *The table in the center of this living room could be moved to one side so that the center can be left open for good Vastu Shastra.*

and is dirt- and dust-free. If the positive energies get trapped or stagnate in a dirty, cluttered room, then this might lead to ill health and financial difficulties. A room that is filled with furniture, or has a very busily designed carpet, very elaborate wallpaper and drapes, excessively bright lighting, or too many multicolored pictures is not conducive to restful energies

The southwest is considered to have the less sought-after energies. It is advisable to keep this section of the house quieter and shut when not in use so that this negative energy stays in the southwestern sector and does not spread to the other parts of the house. This energy can be contained if windows and doors are kept shut as much as possible. Place heavy furniture in the southwestern sector—the furniture will press down on the negative energy, thereby enhancing the positive aspect. If you can raise the floor level in the west, southwest, and south of the house, you will trap the negative energy at the higher level. The positive energy in the lower levels is then free to move. This could be done by building a slightly elevated deck above the existing floor. Take great care, and don't forget to take into account doors, electrical cabling, power outlets, headroom, potential tripping hazards, and any other safety features.

above *A spiral-shaped staircase is not recommended in a house that is built on Vastu Shastra priniples.*

right *The south, west, and southwest areas of your home should be higher and heavier* *than the rest of the house, but take care before making any alterations.*

Some people like to display the heads or bodies of dead, stuffed animals, or have pictures that represent sad, aggressive, destructive energies, or have guns, swords, or other weapons displayed in glass cabinets. Although they may have inherited these artifacts from their forefathers and may attach some sentimental value to them, Vastu Shastra discourages these types of displays. Pictures and objects such as these are not believed to be conducive to healthy living.

You can encourage positive energies by your careful choice of color and lighting within your home. The colors used in different rooms should be chosen to blend harmoniously with the room's function. The bedroom needs restful energies and so light, pastel colors are highly recommended, whereas the living area or kitchen will need brighter more active energy—hence brighter shades are recommended in these rooms.

The kind of lighting you have in a room can create either a stressful or a stress-free environment. Rooms should be adequately lit, and no corner or part of the house should be kept in darkness. Table lamps and dimmer lighting is appropriate in the bedroom, but in a living area spotlights, uplighters, downlighters, and brighter lights will be more suitable so that the family can read and play together with ease. Lights should be placed strategically around the house, ready to serve their intended purpose. The house should be free of damp and should not smell musty—a house that is damp and musty may be the cause of allergies and ill health. A house should be fresh smelling, inviting, warm, and well lit, and it is recommended that you use incense and air fresheners to help clear any stale odors.

left *Lights are used to create a positive energy in a house. Bright lights are recommended in the living area, and dim lights for the bedroom.*

above *If you are trying to follow Vastu Shastra principles you will realize that a stuffed animal head is more appropriate in a museum than a house.*

Indians regard the home as a sacred space, and they do not want to defile it, however small and humble it may be. Because so much dirt and dust can be brought in from the streets, wearing "outside" shoes inside the house is positively discouraged. If you ever visit a house in India, you will find people walking around barefoot or wearing slippers that are intended only for the house and which will never be worn outside. Kitchens and prayer rooms are clean places and it is expected that your body is clean before you enter these rooms either to cook or to pray. In the past, a menstruating woman was considered unclean, and was not allowed into the kitchen.

You do not have to live in a palatial, big home to encourage positive energies—in fact big houses sometimes may have oppressive energies and would be better used as museums and not homes. People who live in palatial homes do not necessarily enjoy a happier life—those who live in good, positive homes do! A clean, well-kept house that is looked after invites a positive feeling and enhances the harmony, health, and wealth of the people living there.

below *Slippers should be worn inside the house—some Hindu homes forbid the wearing of any shoes or slippers in the kitchen.*

MAKING CORRECTIONS

10
QUESTIONS
& ANSWERS

Q I live in a house that is not built along Vastu Shastra principles, but I would like to make the necessary changes. Where do I start?

A If you have lived in this house for some time and are happy there, do not make any changes that will cause unnecessary upheaval. Many of the tips in this chapter can help you create better Vastu Shastra. If you want to do more, then seek professional advice before undertaking any alterations.

Q I have just built a conservatory that has changed the shape of my house from a square to one with an extension in the northeast. Will this affect my good luck?

A In Vastu Shastra the northeast is the most auspicious of all directions since it is believed to be a "gateway to the gods," so your luck will be enhanced. A square or rectangular-shaped extension is preferable to a round or irregular shape. You are very fortunate to live in such a house—this is the most sought-after shape in Vastu Shastra.

Q My apartment is irregular in shape since it has a "missing center." Is this poor Vastu Shastra?

A Vastu Shastra recommends square or rectangular shapes. However, many of our homes were not built in this way and if you live in an apartment that is irregular you have to make do with what you have. Don't consider the shape of the home as a whole, but place the mandala over each room and follow Vastu Shastra principles in designing their layout. Don't forget to keep the center of each individual room free and open, since this is Lord Brahma's area.

Q I want to hide my workstation in the living room. Is there a particular color that I should use to make a partition or screen?

A The screen or partition should be unobtrusive and not be a bright, loud color—it should look as though it belongs to the house and should go with the existing decor. It can incorporate motifs or designs, as long as they are appealing to the eye.

Q We have a vacation home in the country, but live in the city most of the time. Whenever we get time we visit our vacation house to relax and unwind. Should we design either house, or both, according to Vastu Shastra?

A It is entirely your decision. Vastu Shastra is about living in harmony with the environment, and it sounds as if you have two very different environments, both of which will require different treatments.

Q I am building a new house and intend to add a swimming pool. What shape would you suggest that I use?

A The square shape belongs to the earth element and is associated with restful, quiet energies. The round shape belongs to the water element and is associated with aggressive, active energies. A swimming pool needs active energies, so a round-shaped swimming pool is ideal, according to Vastu Shastra.

Q What paint colors should I use to decorate my five-year-old son's bedroom?

A Your son needs to like his room; he also needs bright, active energies. So try to select colors that will suit his age, while keeping his personal likes and dislikes in mind. It is also a good idea to consult him in the process, because he will then feel happier about any changes you make.

Q My bedroom is L-shaped, but I have heard this is not the most auspicious shape. What should I do about this?

A A square-shaped room is preferable in Vastu Shastra. If you are following its principles in your bedroom, you don't have to take drastic steps, such as moving heavy furniture around in order to create square shapes; just use a screen to make two square spaces and then treat both spaces differently. You could use one section for sleeping in and the other as a sitting area.

Q I have tall hedges in the southwest and northeast sections of my garden. I have read that this does not accord with Vastu Shastra principles. Is this true?

A If you want to incorporate Vastu Shastra principles into your garden, then it is recommended that the northeast section of hedge is lower and the southwest section higher. You can trim the northeast hedge so that it is lower by a couple of inches than the one in the southwest sector. Or you could make the difference in height a dramatic feature of your garden.

Q We have a very fancy building, with an atrium in the center, where I think a fountain would look great. Would this be acceptable, according to Vastu Shastra?

A The center of a room or building should be kept as empty as possible because Lord Brahma, the creator of the universe, rules here. Although I am sure that a fountain would look good, this is not recommended in Vastu Shastra.

7

VASTU INSIDE
THE HOME

Take some time to review all the main rooms in your house using Vastu Shastra principles. You will find that there are many, often minor, adjustments that you can make which will greatly enhance the positive harmony of your home. The suggestions below highlight some of the main Vastu Shastra considerations on a room-by-room basis.

above *It is a good idea to display happy pictures of family members in the northeast sector of the house or room.*

LIVING ROOMS

The living room is one of the central rooms in any household. It is where we spend a lot of time relaxing, unwinding, and getting together with the other members of the house and friends. The ideal location for the living room is the north, northwest, or the northeast sector of the home. It should be a room that will stimulate good conversation and should always have a happy and joyful atmosphere. Cheerful flowers, photographs, paintings, rugs, and decorative items can be used to bring life to the room. If you do choose to have pictures or paintings in the room, make sure that they exude soothing, calming, and happy energies. Choose happy family photographs, landscapes, and beautiful buildings— avoid anything that is gloomy or aggressive. It is quite acceptable to have plants in the room, but make sure that they do not have thorns, either on the stems or leaves.

Choose bright and cheerful colors for your living room, but ensure that it is not overbearingly bright. The room should be well lit and you can also use accent lighting to add interest or to highlight pictures, objects, or features. The seating should be comfortable and be arranged so that

left *In Indian homes it is normal to display pictures of ancestors and older members of the family in the living room.*

left *The northeast sector of this room has pictures of various gods and a chair—ideal for meditation and contemplation.*

above *Hi-fi equipment or televisions are ideally placed in the southeast part of a room, since this sector is ruled by the fire element.*

you are encouraging conversation. As always, try to keep the room free of clutter and avoid having unnecessary furniture. Keep furniture away from the doors—you should be able to open doors all the way without their being blocked.

Try to keep the northeast side of the room as clear as is practical. If you also use this room for studying, reading, or any contemplative work, then you could place a chair in the northeast sector, as this is the best location for such activities. The southwest part of the room is where you should place the heavier furniture such as bookcases or cabinets. Your television, with all of its associated components, telephone, and hi-fi equipment are best placed in the southeast section of the room; any electrical equipment is governed by the fire element, which rules the southeast. Try to keep the center of the living room free from furniture; it should be as open and spacious as possible.

above *Your living rooms should be bright, but not too bright. The colors need to be cheerful but not overpowering.*

81

DINING ROOM

Your dining room should be close to the kitchen and the ideal sector for it is the east zone of the house. It should be a welcoming room with comfortable seats— after all, you and your guests might want to spend several hours there.

This room should be conducive to eating good food, drinking fine wine, and enjoying open and animated conversations. It should be a room where people are happy to linger over a meal, rather than gobbling up the food and leaving at the earliest opportunity. Use calm, soothing colors and decorate the north wall with pictures of fruit, which symbolizes abundance. If you wish, you could have a mirror in this room to reflect the food or an attractive outside view. Consider soft, subdued lighting and possibly candles, but ensure that the candles are put out before you retire from the room. .

above *Colors that calm and soothe are ideal for use in the dining room. They should be warm and welcoming.*

below *Candles belong to the fire element and it would therefore be appropriate to place them in the southeast sector of the room.*

above *A square, round, or rectangular table is recommended in Vastu. Tables with sharp edges or irregular shapes should be avoided.*

The table can be square, rectangular, or round. A round table will encourage lively—maybe loud—conversation. If you have a large enough dining room, the table should be placed toward its east section. If you have a bar in the room, the best place for it is on the north side. China and glassware cabinets, which are frequently heavy, should be placed in the southwest section of the room. The dining room should not be adjacent to a bathroom.

STUDY

If you work from home, then the study becomes an important room and, as such, needs careful planning. The west sector of the house is considered to be the best area for study and work. Heavy furniture, such as bookshelves, should be placed in the southwest section of the room. Since north, east, and northeast are believed to bring success and prosperity, try to arrange the room so that you are facing any of these directions when working. Computers, faxes, phones, and so on can be placed in the southeast section, since this section belongs to the fire element, which governs electrical equipment. Place your desk in the south section of the room to tap into leadership and power attributes associated with this direction. Avoid putting your desk in the northwest section of the room, as the air element, which encourages restlessness and movement, rules this sector and you might find yourself not so ready to do work that needs attention or long hours.

left *Computers, faxes, and other electrical equipment should be placed in the southeast sector of your study. Ensure that the center of the room is kept clutter-free.*

Your study should be a room that can foster inspiration, but the decor must not be too busy. You can have pictures and objects that relate to the type of work or activity carried out in the room. Keep the workspace free of clutter and dust and keep only the books and materials that you need in the room. The room should have bright— but not loud—colors. You want to bring positive energy into the room to encourage concentration.

83

BEDROOM

This is the room to which you retire at the end of a long and weary day, so it should be comfortable, relaxing, and cozy. It should be a room that will help you to sleep. A bedroom in the southwest sector of the house is the Vastu Shastra ideal. This is considered the most auspicious sector for a bedroom, and the breadwinner should sleep there if possible. Other family members can sleep i n other sectors; since east is the source of enlightenment and inspiration, it is a good sector for a child's bedroom. If you don't want guests to stay too long, try putting your guest bedroom in the northwest area, as this direction belongs to the air element and denotes restlessness! Try not to have a bedroom in the center of the house.

Because in Vastu Shastra the north and east are considered as the directions from which the most positive energies originate, it is good to face these directions when you sit up in bed, especially first thing in the morning, so the head of your bed should be at the southern or western end of your bedroom. The bed itself should be in the southwest part of the room if that is practical. Heavy furniture, such as wardrobes and storage cabinets, should be in the west, southwest, and south, while the lighter furniture, such as a dressing table or chair, can be in the northeast, north, or east part of the room. Try to keep the center of the room free for Lord Brahma—of course, if you have a small room and a large bed, this won't be possible.

left A bedroom is ideally placed in the southwest sector of the house. The center of the room should be free of any furniture if possible.

You should ensure that your feet do not face the door, when in bed—if it is unavoidable, place a screen between the foot of the bed and the door. If your arrangement means that your feet are facing a religious image, you should move the image to another place. Do not sleep with your head immediately under an overhead object – for instance, under an exposed beam.

Soft pastel colors are recommended for walls, drapes, and soft furnishings. Lighting should not be too bright or harsh; a dimmer switch is a good feature for this room. Spotlights are not appropriate in here, but soft uplighters or downlighters can be used. Although candles are great for atmosphere, remember that any naked flame in a home is an inherent danger. If you want to listen to music in bed, the best place for the equipment in the southeast section of the room. If you want to keep jewelry or valuables in the bedroom, place them in an appropriate strong box that should be kept in the room's northern sector.

above *The northwest sector is ruled by the air element, whose attributes are mobility and restlessness. It is therefore ideal for the guest bedroom.*

SUN RISE

East is where the sun rises. It is the beginning of a new day and therefore signifies new hopes and desires and is full of promises. It represents the young and strong. It is an "upward direction" and an uplifting one—it is the "zenith." West is where the sun sets and it signifies decline, the end of the day's activity and the beginning of darkness, of rest and quiet—it is the "nadir" point. Because it is opposite to east, there is always a pull and an attraction between the two—the pull or attraction between heavenly aspiration and physical appetites, desires, needs, and worldly appetites.

left *You can use various shades of the recommended colors to enhance an element in a given room.*

KITCHEN

According to Vastu Shastra, the kitchen is a "wet room" and because it is the room where food is cooked, it belongs in the southeast sector of the house, where the fire element rules. This part of the house should receive adequate fresh air and natural light to keep it hygienically dry and clean. The stove should be placed in such a way that you face east when cooking; you will then attract all of the blessings from the east while preparing food.

The southeast section of the kitchen, which is ruled by fire, is the ideal part of the room for the placement of electrical equipment such as microwaves, ovens, toasters, and kettles. The water elements—sink, dishwasher, and washing machine—are

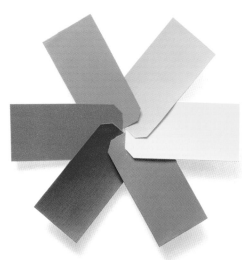

right *The colors shown here are best kept for kitchen accessories and decoration details, keep the main surfaces plain, cheerful, but not too bold.*

above *Since east is the source of all positive and beneficial energies, it is advisable to face east while cooking, and lay out the kitchen accordingly.*

ideally placed along the north wall or in the northern area. The heaviest equipment in the kitchen is often the refrigerator and freezer and these should be placed in the west or southwest section or wall. A breakfast table can be placed along the east wall. Try to leave the center of the kitchen as free as possible. The kitchen should be well lit and decorated with bright and cheerful colors. Often it is the second "central room" in a house, so it should have a homely atmosphere. To add interest to the room, you can grow herbs on the kitchen windowsill, have a few plants, cheerful gingham drapes, a vibrant tablecloth, and colorful pots and pans. Ensure that you have a good ventilation system that will chase the cooking smells away.

Kitchens should never be located in the center of the house, which should be kept free, nor should they be located near a bathroom or the main entrance to the house.

above *A cooker in the center of the kitchen is not recommended in Vastu Shastra.*

left *Colors can be introduced into the kitchen by using brightly colored pots, pans, crockery, and table cloths.*

87

BATHROOM

Bathrooms are also "wet rooms" and are best located in the east or the south sector of the house. Bathrooms in the northeast sector of the home are frowned upon since this sector is the "gateway to the gods." A bathroom should not be next to a "prayer room" or a kitchen, nor should it be located in the center of the house. The colors used in the bathroom should be refreshing and pleasing – blues, greens, or whites (not on its own). Mirrors can be located on the north or east walls. Toilets should be in the south section and bathtubs, since they are the heaviest, in the southwest part of the bathroom. No religious images or books should be placed in or near the bathroom or facing it. Keep the bathroom clean and dry. If you want to have candles in the bathroom you can place them in the southeast section—make sure you extinguish them before you leave the room. En suite bathrooms are difficult to accommodate because there can be so many of them—if you have any, then try to follow the above guidelines as much as is practical, and ensure that you keep the bathroom door shut whenever possible.

left *Bathrooms need maximum sunlight to keep then dry and hygienically clean— hence it is ideal to locate them in the south or east sector of the house.*

left *Bathrooms need colors that are refreshing and cleansing—blues and greens, any of their shades are perfect.*

left *When choosing colors remember that different shades of one color can be used to great effect.*

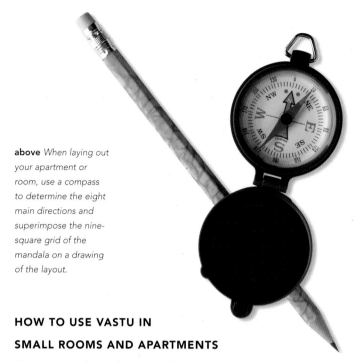

above When laying out your apartment or room, use a compass to determine the eight main directions and superimpose the nine-square grid of the mandala on a drawing of the layout.

HOW TO USE VASTU IN SMALL ROOMS AND APARTMENTS

This section tells you how to apply Vastu Shastra to an apartment where size dictates that rooms might combine functions. Take a compass and locate the eight directions—north, south, east, west, northeast, northwest, southeast, and southwest. Draw a rough layout of your apartment on a sheet of paper—at least 8 inches by 11 inches. Draw your plan so that the rooms are the right proportions to each other—show the locations of your doors and windows. Next, draw a grid of nine equal squares (three by three) on top of the sketched apartment and assign a direction to each square—the central zone is, of course, the square in the middle. Make sure that you include the entire apartment inside the grid.

You can now see which room is in which sector or sectors. Walk around the apartment and mark the layout of the fittings and furniture on your sketch. You also need to match the elements with the square on the layout as you go along. Don't forget that the elements are also associated with a color, a function, and so on.

THE LINES IN A GRID

A line in the grid that travels from South to North is considered as the "Fire Line"—the line flows in an upward direction with north of the grid at the top and south of the grid at the bottom. The line that links them together has an upward flow and is a representation of divine truth and inspiration. The vertical lines in any picture or image are considered to denote serenity and peace.

An East-West orientation is considered to be the "Water Line"—the lines flow in a horizontal direction, a restful position. The horizontal lines in an image denote sorrow or loss.

The diagonal lines are those in the grid that run from northeast-southwest or southeast-northwest and are considered to be "Wind Lines." These lines have dynamic, aggressive movements and all of them meet and converge at one point, which is the central point of the grid called the "bindu." These lines in an image or picture denote aggression and action.

The "bindu" is the place from where a person draws their strength and aspirations and gets their focus—when they become detached from this center point, they becomes less focused and restless and are believed to lack direction and become disconnected from the soul or "atman." The "bindu" therefore represents a person's inner consciousness and is represented in images by the lotus flower. Any damage to the "bindu" is believed to lead to havoc.

Similarly, a building's central area, the courtyard or "angan," was very important and an empty space in the center of a room is essential since it is the focus for all energy and must be kept clean and empty.

Start at the entrance. When you live in an apartment, you cannot do too much to change what is outside your own set of rooms, but you can at least ensure that the outside of your own apartment is always clean and tidy—it might not be your job to do it, but you will gain the benefit. Is the entrance to your own apartment well-lit, clean, painted, and welcoming? Does the door open into the apartment? Is it a solid door? Is it larger than other doors in the apartment? Is it in good condition and well painted? Does it have your name or number displayed prominently? This is where the energies come from and you will want to ensure that all the energy entering your home is positive. In India, people have a picture of gods displayed at their house entrances; they do it to seek blessings from the gods and they also believe that this picture protects the house from negative energies and forces. Some even paint the sign "om" on their front entrances. Others might place a garland of fresh flowers there.

left Bringing fresh flowers into your home, particularly at the entrance, can usher in the positive energies you want to attract.

below A brightly lit entrance looks attractive and welcoming, but the main door of the building should be wood, and not contain glass.

right The entrance to your home is very important—it is traditional in Vastu to have the symbol "Om" by your door.

above *A treasure chest can hold anything of sentimental value. They are ideally placed in the north sector of the house or room.*

THE EIGHT SECTORS

The layout that you have drawn of the apartment is a rough representation of your home. How would you describe the shape? The ideal shape would be square or even rectangle. An L- or T-shaped apartment is not ideal since it is believed to have missing energies, but if you are living in one like that, don't worry—just consider it as two separate areas and work both of them separately. Don't forget you can use furniture, screens, and plants as separators.

Now consider each room and mark out its directional zone and the compass direction each wall is facing. The north section of the room is governed by the water element and ruled by the god of wealth and health. A water feature in this section is believed to enhance wealth. You can also have your "treasure chest" here, in which you might keep valuable items—not necessarily of great monetary value but perhaps of great sentimental value (for example, letters, pictures, or family photographs). This section of the room is also an ideal place for your medical kit. The north is also related to the color blue—if you wish, you can paint this part of the wall or room in a shade of blue, or instead you might choose to have a picture, a rug, or drape of this color to enhance the element in this section of the apartment.

above *The ideal front door according to Vastu Shastra should be located in the north, east, or northeast section of the house.*

right *Sometimes it can be difficult to make changes. Cheap alternatives, such as colored throws, work well and are still good Vastu Shastra.*

The northeast section is "the gateway to the gods" and is believed to be the source of all positive energies. The god of purity rules this section. If the apartment has windows here, keep them open as much as possible to let the positive energies into the apartment, but make sure you are protected from burglars, and if you live above the lowest floor and have children, make sure that they cannot climb out. This section of the wall or apartment should be kept clear, leaving as much open space as is both possible and practical. If space dictates that you have to use the area for furniture, then try to place lighter and lower furniture here. If you have any kind of religious belief, it is good to display icons or pictures in this area. It is also the place to have a chair to use when reading or meditating. The color yellow represents this direction and painting this part of your home with a shade of yellow will enhance the energy. If you do not want to paint the walls yellow, you can introduce the color through accessories.

The south section is ruled by the earth element and its color is also yellow. The god of justice and duty is the ruler. If you wish to enhance the energy emanating from here, you can place earthen objects here, like porcelain vases. If you have a child, this section of the room is considered to be ideal for his or her bed. This is one of the best directions to sleep, and your head should face south so that you face north when you wake.

above *The northeast section of the room or house contains positive energies and this section is ideal for sitting quietly. This part of the room should include touches of yellow.*

top right *There are various tones of yellow so it shouldn't be too difficult to find at least one that you can live with.*

right *The south section of the house is ruled by the earth element, represented by the color yellow. It is therefore a good idea to incorporate yellow and shades of yellow into this sector.*

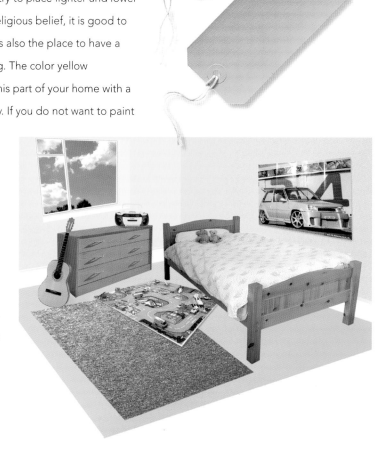

The southeast direction belongs to the god of fire and its color is red. It is considered the ideal location for any electrical equipment, such as televisions, microwaves, and kettles . It is an excellent section of the living room in which to locate a heating device—real or artificial.

The west direction is represented by the air element and ruled by the god of rain, river, oceans, and water. The west sector is considered ideal for the dining table or the breakfast bar; indeed, Vastu Shastra recommends facing east as much as possible while eating.

The god of misery rules the southwest direction. Place any heavy furniture in this section of the apartment to stop the energy of the god from flowing into the room. If you have windows on this side, keep them shut as much as possible. This direction should be kept quiet, so avoid placing music-playing equipment here. Having a bed here is also considered good since the weight will press down on the negative energy, thereby enhancing the positive. This section of the room or apartment is best for the breadwinner's bed with the bed facing east–west, or north–south. On awakening, you should be facing east or north to get most benefit. It is also the direction that "belongs" to our ancestors, so it is the best place to display any pictures of departed relatives.

below *The ideal color for your kitchen is red, but red may be a little too hard to handle so just include red accessories.*

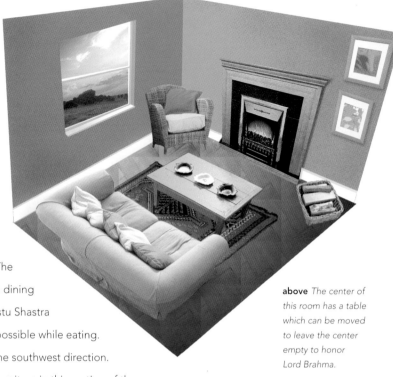

above *The center of this room has a table which can be moved to leave the center empty to honor Lord Brahma.*

left *A directions color need not over-power— you can choose soft furnishings in the color rather than paint all the walls.*

93

right *The sun is the source of all energies, and it is considered auspicious to have an office or house that faces east.*

The east direction is where the sun rises. It is governed by the fire element and is ruled by the god of power. It is the ideal sector for the location of a bathroom.

The room should get maximum sunlight—if it doesn't, consider adding more artificial light here. Try and face east when eating, cooking, studying, and praying. Facing this direction when doing any such work is believed to bring enlightenment and happiness.

The god of wind rules the northwest. If you work from home, maybe in a "cottage industry" making artifacts, or painting and designing, you should keep your "finished goods" in this section of the apartment. The element in this part of the apartment is air, which also governs activity, mobility, and movement, and which should encourage the quick sale of goods.

LEARNING VASTU

Traditional artists and craftsmen lived in closed communities and the rules of design and construction were passed on by word of mouth from father to son or teacher to student. Writing was a rare art and one had to memorize the rules.

below *It is a good idea to place a work table so that it faces east when undertaking creative work.*

VASTU PURUSHA MANDALA

In addition, remember to adhere to the following general Vastu Shastra principles, and you will maximize the positive energy in your apartment:

• Your windows must never be blocked, as they need to let fresh air and light into the apartment.

• Any pictures that you display should be happy and bright and of a size that is appropriate to the size of room—not so large that they dominate.

• Furniture should always be arranged in such a way that the energy flows easily, and is not blocked by any unnecessary items. Heavy furniture should be placed in the southwest, west, and south of the room as much as possible.

• Try to keep the center of all rooms free of any furniture or clutter, if possible.

• Your curtains, rugs, and cushions should be cheerful and bright but not so bright that you or others are uncomfortable.

• Try to arrange your home so that you do not work, sleep, study, or cook immediately under an exposed beam.

• Do not have thorn-bearing plants like cacti in the house.

• Incense sticks, mood candles, and scented candles will all add to the ambience of the apartment and are best used in the east of the room. Always ensure that you put them out before retiring for the night.

above *Lighter furniture is ideal in the east, north, and northeast section of the room to enhance the flow of positive energies to the other sectors of the house.*

As the saying goes, our house is our castle, whether it is a huge mansion or a bijou residence. It not only provides shelter, but in its familiar surroundings we can relax and unwind. Whatever the size of your home, it should be bright, smell fresh, and be clean. You might not have too much choice about its size or location, but you do have a choice about how you will look after it. Irrespective of size, dust, dirt, and clutter obstruct the free travel of positive energies and can cause them to stagnate—in much the same way that the water in a junk-filled pond stagnates. Keep your home spick and span—let the energies do their work.

VASTU INSIDE THE HOME

10
QUESTIONS & ANSWERS

Q My bathroom is in the northeast sector of my studio apartment. How can I use Vastu Shastra principles there?

A Don't worry that this is not the ideal sector of your home for a bathroom. Simply concentrate on your living area and use Vastu Shastra principles there. Unless we build a new house, most of us are unlikely to have a home that follows Vastu Shastra guidelines 100 percent.

Q I make candles and work from home, with my workshop in the northwest sector. Is that good Vastu Shastra?

A The northwest section of the house is ruled by Vayu, the wind, and is associated with mobility. So work that needs concentration should not be carried out in this sector. If you are making items to sell, however, this sector is ideal—being fast-moving and fast-selling. Keep your finished candles in the northwest section of the workshop to ensure a quick sale.

Q I have both dried and silk flowers in my house. Does Vastu Shastra approve of displaying them, as I understand that feng shui frowns on their use.

A Vastu Shastra does not prohibit the display of dried plants as long as they are clean and dust-free. In feng shui, however, dried flowers are considered to have yin energies, which should be less conspicuous in a home.

Q I love the scent of incense and use it in "space-clearing." Which sector of the house should I light it in?

A You can use incense in any part of your house, although the northeast sector is most auspicious because this represents the "gateway to gods." This section must be kept clean, clear, and sweet-smelling to enhance the flow of positive energies to the rest of the house. If you are space-clearing it is good to start from the northeast and work clockwise around the house.

Q I have a box of mementos, in which I keep personal letters and cards that I have received over the years. Which part of my bedroom should I keep these in?

A According to Vastu principles, it is good to keep these in the north part of your bedroom, as this sector is where you should keep your treasures or valuable items. Of course this doesn't guarantee their security; and you must always ensure that your house is secure and protected from theft. It is important to keep safety in mind whenever you start to use Vastu Shastra guidelines in your house.

Q My bedroom is in the north of the house, where I have a picture of a waterfall on the north wall. Is this acceptable in Vastu Shastra, as it is not recommended in feng shui?

A According to Vastu Shastra, the north is ruled by the element water, so a water feature here will promote wealth luck. In feng shui, the element water also rules the north and is recommended here, but a water feature is not considered beneficial in a bedroom. You should try not to mix the two practices; each has benefits, but you must stick to one.

Q In which direction does the "purusha" or cosmic man in the Vastu Purusha Mandala have to be placed?

A The Vastu Purusha Mandala is a grid used to design a house according to Vastu Shastra principles. If you are interested in designing your living or workspace according these principles, then you have to try to follow the rules. The purusha is always placed with his head in the northeast, irrespective of the shape, size, or location of the property.

Q I travel a lot in my job and it is very hard to practise Vastu Shastra. What do you recommend that I do?

A You can use Vastu Shastra principles in your normal day-to-day life, whether you are working, sleeping, or eating. All you have to do is try as far as possible to face the recommended directions while carrying out each task. Be conscious of your environment while you are doing so, and don't worry unduly if you cannot face the correct direction.

Q I live in a house that is 250 years old. The bedroom ceiling has exposed beams—in fact I and my partner sleep under one. Does this bring bad luck?

A Exposed beams were part of the building tradition of that era and they do add character to a house. But sleeping, working, studying, or eating directly under a beam is not auspicious Vastu Shastra. You should move your bed away; if that is not possible, then "dress" the beam with thin cheesecloth to create a canopy effect—the beam will then become less harmful.

Q I have a two-bedroom apartment. Which is the best direction for me, as the breadwinner of the household, to use as a bedroom?

A The south sector is ruled by the earth element and by Yama, the lord of justice and duty. It is considered to be a good sector for a bedroom. The southwest sector is ruled by the ancestors' luck and is far more preferable for a bedroom for the owner of the house, since it is believed that by sleeping here he or she will gain the wisdom of the ancestors.

8

VASTU IN THE GARDEN

Earth is one of the important elements in Vastu Shastra—together with the heat and light of the sun, and the oxygen and nitrogen of the air, it sustains life. Vastu Shastra emphasizes the importance of living in an area where the soil is rich and fertile. Good soil, combined with heat, light, oxygen, and nitrogen, is an essential requirement for growing food—both for humans and livestock—and cultivating herbs for medicinal needs. The land should have a gentle slope that encourages good drainage, thus helping the plants to flourish.

If you are fortunate enough to live in a home with a garden, then treat the garden with the same care that you lavish on your home. As with the house, the well-designed and well-tended garden will bring benefit to all of the household members. Unfortunately, open spaces in many large cities are all too often seen as a good place to dump unwanted furniture, cars, and much more. Frequently plants, hedges, and trees are untended and left to grow wild. It is a sad fact that these derelict areas are an all too common feature of many cities—even if the price of property in these areas is lower, avoid seeking a home in such places. These neighborhoods are unappealing to the senses and any good, positive energy will find it difficult to survive in them.

In many cases the front of your house is the first thing that any passers-by will see, since it is the place that has maximum exposure to the road. Remember that, for a passer-by, a single

above *Plants that flower are considered particularly auspicious in Vastu Shastra.*

left *Grounds that give support to animals and vegetation are considered to have good Vastu Shastra.*

right *The front garden should be well tended and kept trimmed back—greenery should not be overpoweringly tall in front of the house.*

glance at the front of a house will be sufficient for them to form an opinion of not only the house but also the people living in it. If you have a garden in the front of your house, it should have the same appeal as the front of your house.

If you have two gardens—usually one in front of the house and one behind—consider the two spaces as different entities. The front garden might be just a small open space—if this is the case, do not crowd it. Keep this space open and free by avoiding having too many plants or trees. While you might not have sufficient space to create a meandering path that leads from the front gate to the main door (considered an effective way of directing the energies into your home), you can still lay tiles in a meandering pattern to create the desired effect.

When planning or designing your garden, continue to keep in mind the importance of the various directions, the several elements, colors, principles, and the gods that rule each sector. Try to incorporate some of the principles that you have learned for your house into the planning of your garden. A garden designed with Vastu Shastra principles need not be expensive or elaborate—simplicity and balance are the keys. It can still be beautiful and a joyful place in which to relax.

below *A meandering, rather than a straight, front path will slow down the rush of energies from the gate to the main door.*

left *Try to have a low-maintenance garden that does not need too much looking after and is therefore easy to keep tidy.*

99

NORTHEAST

The northeast is the gateway to the gods, so keep this entry clear of all obstructions. You may not be able to do anything about what is on the other side of your fence line, but you can always look after your own side. Tall trees in this section of the garden are not appropriate. This section of the garden should be fairly open; if you want to plant here, choose the shorter varieties of shrubs, hedges, and trees. If it is possible, and looks good, try to create a little sunken area in this section of the garden—it will act as a receptacle, or reservoir, where the positive energy can gather before meandering off into the house. It doesn't have to be very deep, but make sure it is well drained, as you don't want a deep puddle in the winter! Always keep the northeast section of your garden neat, clean, and free from clutter—so no garden gnomes, garden furniture, or rock gardens.

If you wish to, you can grow flowers or fruit-bearing plants in this section, but always avoid having any thorny plants here. If you like to spend a lot of time in your garden reading or relaxing, a garden chair would be appropriate here. As with the house, the northeast is a great place for exercising, or doing yoga, contemplative work, or meditation. Bearing this in mind, you might find that a lawned area could fit well into your plans.

above *A rockery is ideal in the southwest section, and a water feature is best placed in the north sector.*

left *The northeast section of the garden should be lower than the southwest. Tall trees and plants are ideal in the southwest.*

EAST

The sun god Surya rules here. This part of your garden should receive sunlight during the earlier part of the day (although this is not always possible, especially if your neighbors' tall trees block out the light). It is therefore a good place to grow plants that like sunlight—provided that the plants are right for the climatic zone and season, and that other conditions such as soil and drainage are right, they will bloom and flourish here.

Fire rules the east, so this is a good place for a barbecue—cook here, but eat in another part of the garden.

Tall trees and thorn-bearing plants are discouraged here. Red is the color for the sector, so choose red-flowering plants such as tulips, geraniums, and dahlias—avoid thorn-bearing roses. Although the emphasis for the sector is red, there is no reason why you should not have other colors as well.

SOUTH

Lord Yama, lord of duty, death, and justice rules here. This section is associated with the sense of smell and the color yellow . Because it is ruled by the earth element, this is a prime location for earthenware or stoneware objects, such as statues or rock features. Grow tall trees here, but don't plant them too close to the house. Ensure that they do not dwarf the house by trimming them regularly. Look for a predominance of fragrant plants and flowers with yellow blooms—you could choose a beautiful yellow, sweet-scented rose, since thorns are not disallowed here.

below A barbecue is ideally placed in the east sector of the garden since it is ruled by the fire element.

above The south sector of the garden is ruled by the earth element, and is the ideal place for any heavy statues made of earthenware.

left The east, north, and northeast should be kept free of any thorn-bearing plants, such as roses and cacti.

101

SOUTHEAST

Lord Agni, god of fire rules here, and so it is another good place for your barbecue. Plants that thrive on strong sunlight, will flourish here. Keep this section fairly low and free from any thorny plants.

WEST

This section belongs to Varuna, god of rain and water. Because it is bathed in the sun's weaker rays, it is a suitable place for plants that need less light. A water feature here is good Vastu Shastra—flowing from west to east. Pay attention to how you dispose of the water. Having barbecued your food elsewhere, you can bring it here for your al fresco dining!

SOUTHWEST

The southwest is ruled by the earth element and by Niritti, the god of misery. A rockery is appropriate here, or a collection of pebbles and stones. This is a suitable area for objects made of porcelain or decorative earthen garden features. Avoid having statues with missing heads or limbs here—or anywhere in the garden.

This section of your garden can be the highest. Lay down decking to raise the level, or build steps and grading to create higher and lower levels. Higher levels should be in the west, southwest, or south section of the garden only, with the northeast, east, and north sections always lower. The southwest is ideal for garden seating. Don't forget that the best directions for seating to face are east, north, or northeast.

top *Place a body of water in the north sector. Ensure that it is kept clean and flowing.*

above *Keep the center of the garden free and empty of any trees or garden furniture.*

below *The earth element rules in the southwest, where a rockery will help in enhancing good, positive energies.*

102

NORTH

Kubera, the god of health and wealth, rules the north. The water element rules here and, as one of the Vastu Shastra beliefs is that a water feature in the north will encourage wealth and prosperity, you are certainly advised to add one here. Your water feature could be a fountain, a pond, or even (if you have the room, weather, and budget) a swimming pool. If you want to create a little artificial flowing water feature here, design it so that the water will flow from south to north. Always make sure that the water does not become stagnant or dirty. If you have a pond, you could grow water-bearing plants, and keep fish appropriate to the climate. Don't forget that even fish need food, so you might have to add food to supplement nature's supply. Vegetables and fruits will thrive in this section, as will fragrant plants and shrubs that will enhance the beauty of the garden. Avoid thorn-bearing plants here. This is another section of the garden that should be kept low, so tall trees are not encouraged.

NORTHWEST

Lord Vayu, the god of wind, rules the northwest section, and the ruling element is air. This section of the garden is ideal for broad-leaved trees, so long as they are kept well trimmed and are not too close to the house. A very tall or dense tree that is situated too close to the house could dwarf the house and also cut out the light. A shadow cast by a tree onto a house is considered inauspicious according to Vastu Shastra, but it may also present a real safety hazard.

above *Tall, heavy garden plants and trees are ideal in the south, southwest, and western sectors.*

right *A fountain in the north sector of the garden enhances wealth luck.*

far right *The center of the garden should be kept free and empty, except for a well-maintained lawn.*

THE ESTABLISHMENT OF A CENTRAL COURTYARD

The center of your garden, both in the front or the back of the house, is ruled by Lord Brahma, and should be kept free and open as possible. Use the Vastu Purusha mandala to determine the optimum size. You can have a lawn here, but it is important to keep it clean and trim it regularly. Alternatively, you could pave the area. Whatever you choose to do, leave this area bare; do not plant any trees or have water features, furniture, or ornaments of any type here.

VERANDAS

A veranda is a roofed gallery or terrace that runs along the front or side of a building. These open spaces are structurally attached to the house, but are still open to nature. As with the garden, a veranda in the east can be used for plants that require lots of sunlight. Verandas are not recommended in the west, south, and southwest section of the house. If you do have a veranda here, you could counterbalance the inauspicious location by adding a rock feature.

BALCONIES

A balcony is a structure that projects from a building wall, supported by pillars or strong brackets and surrounded with railings or a balustrade. Balconies are ideal places to grow plants—simply follow the same guidlines as when planting for the garden. If the balcony is small, hanging baskets might be worth considering.

above Create a seating area in the east, north, or northeast part of the garden. Try to face north or east while eating.

below Window plants and hanging baskets will create a burst of color and enhance the beauty of a building.

PATIO

A patio is a paved area usually adjoining a house, where outdoor meals can be served. A great location for this is in the southwest. The southwest corner is a good location for placing heavy outdoor dining furniture perhaps made of heavy wood or wrought iron. Heavy earthenware pots and plants or a rock garden can also be designed for this area. Since the southwest belongs to the earth element a body of water or a water feature is not recommended in this corner.

TREES

There should never be any trees immediately in front of the main door or entrance. Trees must be looked after and trimmed to make sure that they do not become dangerous or overpower the house by their sheer size. They should never be planted too close to the house—you do not want gutters blocked by falling leaves, tiles displaced by overhanging branches, or foundations undermined by spreading roots. Fruit-bearing trees, a natural source of food, are always encouraged. Trees that have thorns or ones that ooze sap when cut are not favored. Any trees in the northeast, north, and east should be shorter than the trees in the south, west, and southwest. Trees should never be planted in the center of the garden.

above *According to Vastu Shastra, it is recommended that your garden contains flower- or fruit-bearing plants or trees.*

below *Trees should be trimmed back when they spread out too much or get too tall.*

105

above *A house or building should preferably have two gates, one at the back and the other at the front of the property.*

GATES

The preferred location for gates leading to and from the house are in the north, northeast, or east of the property. Gates in the northeast, east, and north section should be slightly lower in height than any gates you have in the southwest, west, and south of the property. The recommended colors for gates are blue in the north, red in the east, yellow in the south and northeast, gray in the west and southeast, black in the southwest, and white in the northwest.

Two gates are recommended, provided your property is suitable. Locate them in the front and at the back of the property. Try to ensure that any gates are not aligned in a straight line in relation to each other—they should be staggered so that energy does not rush through the plot.

Front gates should be protected, well kept, and looked after. They should also display the number or name of the house in bold, easy-to-read letters. There should be no obstruction immediately in front of the gate—no puddles of dirty or stagnant water, no trees, or lamp-posts.

above *Gates can be ornate so that the opening to your property is welcoming. Paths should wind their way to your door—the careful placing of pots and plants can achieve this, and look beautiful to the visitor.*

left *Only grow plants if you have the time to look after them and to keep the garden both tidy and attractive.*

CHOOSING PLANTS AND SHRUBS

Try to avoid having thorn-bearing plants and shrubs, particularly in the north, northeast, and east sections. If you have limited space, say: a small garden, porch, or patio, your plants can be grown in containers made of different materials and different colors and shapes. Plants such as geraniums, pansies, lobelia, and petunias can also be grown in hanging baskets. Remember to "dead-head" flowers and— particularly with those in tubs and baskets—water and feed them regularly. Having lots of plants does not mean that you improve the Vastu Shastra, keep only what is easy to look after. If you don't have the time to do the gardening avoid plants that need a lot of maintenance.

left *You can use pots of various sizes, shapes, designs, and colors to enhance the beauty of the garden.*

107

PLANTING

NORTH

Because the lord of health rules this section, herbs and medicinal plants are best grown here. Plants such as the lotus and the water lily can grow in the pond in the north section of your garden. Because the sector color is blue, try and choose blue-flowering plants here, such as the baby blue forget-me-not, the iris, or even the humble bluebell.

NORTHEAST

This is the section that is ruled by the lord of purity. There are no particular plants recommended for this area, although white-flowering plants would be appropriate. Low and sweet-smelling varieties are suggested.

EAST

The ruling planet is the sun. Plants that thrive in sunlight, such as dahlias and geraniums, are ideal here. Try to choose low-growing plants. Ferns are also a good choice.

SOUTHEAST

Lord Agni, the lord of fire, and the planet Venus rule this section. Recommended colors for plants in this section are shades of red and also white.

WEST

Lord Varuna, lord of the rain, rules here. You can use this section of the garden for planting taller plants and shrubs that will contain the negative energies and prevent them from straying to the other sections of the garden. Heavy potted plants are ideal here. Dense foliage and shrubs will also work as a natural way of creating a private area.

NORTHWEST

Lord Vayu, the lord of wind, rules here. Here you can have plants such as pansies and crocus. Dense foliage is good too.

SOUTH

The element earth and the color yellow come into effect here. Begonias, mimosa, and marigold can add a splash of golden yellow here. You can also grow plants with exotic smells, such as jasmine and perfumed lilies.

SOUTHWEST

This is the ideal place for taller plants and shrubs. You should encourage dense foliage and wild flowers as well as flowering vines such as morning glory, wisteria, and canary creeper here.

VASTU GARDENING PRINCIPLES—A SUMMARY

Do not aim to cover every inch of the garden with greenery and
shrubbery—as always in Vastu Shastra, aspire to keeping a balance,
even in your garden. Decide what types of trees, plants, shrubs,
herbs, and vegetables that you want and then, with
the help of this chapter, set about designing your
garden. Whether you are working on an
existing planted garden or are setting out to
create a fresh one, always ensure that your
plants are not neglected. They should be well
looked-after and, when necessary, they should
be dead-headed, pruned, and trimmed.
Regular pruning will encourage new growth
and lead to healthier plants.

below *A garden that
has lots of plants may
look attractive, but it
will need a lot of money,
time, and dedication
to maintain.*

You don't have to have a lavish garden—it might just
be one or two well-maintained potted plants. Remember that it
should suit your needs and your particular budget and schedule.
There is no point in investing in so many plants that you cannot
properly maintain them, or even look at them. If you don't have the
time and can't afford a gardener, then don't plant anything that you
cannot look after yourself.

left *A well-kept garden
that has few plants and
trees is easy to
maintain and can also
look attractive.*

Pay special attention to your front garden. If the front section of
your garden is not square in shape, try to create a square
area within it. Keep the path that leads from the
front gate to the entrance of the house free
from overhanging plants and bushes. You
should never have to maneuver or dodge your
way between the plants to get to the house. Do
not plant any tree or large bush directly in front of your main door,
and try to ensure that the path that leads from the gate through

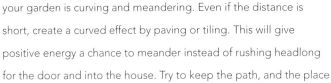

your garden is curving and meandering. Even if the distance is short, create a curved effect by paving or tiling. This will give positive energy a chance to meander instead of rushing headlong for the door and into the house. Try to keep the path, and the place near the gate or the door, free of any thorn-bearing plants, or plants with prickly leaves, such as holly.

Try to have some plants—they don't have to be tall—along the sides of the path to accentuate its meandering shape.

If there are substantial shrubs or trees in the front of the house, keep them at a sufficient distance to avoid overpowering the house. Remember that trees can also cut off the light to the house, while overhanging branches and creeping root systems can damage roofs and foundations.

If the front of your house faces northeast, avoid having any trees, large bushes, or a hedge, at the front. On the other hand, if the front of the house is north-facing, this is a good place for a water feature, but do not have an overpoweringly large water feature that might dominate the front—it should be in balance and suitably proportioned with the size of the house. Also, you must ensure that your water feature is not too close to your front door or right in front of it.

Finally, remember that, if you are looking for a low-maintenance garden, a mix of wild flowers such as daisies can be grown easily and are perfect for a relaxed approach to gardening.

above *A meandering path helps the energies to linger and slow down on their way to the front door. Water features should be small so as not to obstruct the energy.*

above *Plants that have prickly leaves should not be planted in the north, east, or northeast section of the garden.*

left *If plants are allowed to grow wild they will cut off the light from your house, overpowering the front entrance.*

above *Plants can be put in pots of various shapes and sizes, create an attractive "layered" effect.*

THE IMPORTANCE OF A HERB GARDEN

For centuries herbs were grown for their healing powers or for their flavoring—adding interest and pleasure to food. You can still have access to nature's gifts by having your own herb garden. If you grow your own herbs, you will be able to use natural remedies for minor ailments, such as sunburn and wasp stings, while herbs such as thyme, mint, marjoram, and bay will add fresh flavors to your home cooking. In addition, herbs will suffuse your garden with colors and aromas. The northeast, north, or east parts of your garden are the recommended zones for planting herbs. If you don't have the space for a herb garden, why not try growing some in small containers on your kitchen windowsill? Read up on the various herbs—understand what they look like and use them where and as instructed. Do not become a do-it-yourself medic—if you are sick, do not try to cure yourself, seek the advice of a medical practitioner. We are fortunate to live in an age when our scientific knowledge gives us the benefit of drugs and antibiotics to cure many of the illnesses which befall us. Finally, remember that not all plants are edible. If you do not have the space for a herb garden or are too busy and have no time to grow or maintain one don't worry. It is far better not to have a garden than to have one that is unkempt and uncared for. It is very important that you make sure that your garden is kept neat and tidy.

below *Herbs will not only suffuse your garden with aromas, they also enhance your cooking and have great medicinal value.*

111

VASTU IN THE GARDEN

10 QUESTIONS & ANSWERS

Q According to feng shui, one should not use pot pourri. Does the same thing apply to Vastu Shastra?

A According to Vastu Shastra you can use pot pourri in your house and get the benefit of its pleasing aromas. You should not try to equate feng shui with Vastu Shastra: while their aims are similar, they work on totally different principles.

Q We like having our dinners in the garden during the summer and fall. Do you have any tips on lighting for the garden?

A There is no specific Vastu requirement. You can use uplighters or downlighters all round the edge of the garden, or have candles or lanterns. Whatever you use, make sure that they are installed safely. Try and keep your dining table in the east section of the garden, if possible, and face north, east, or northeast while eating, because these are the directions that have positive energies.

Q I want to put a hammock in my back garden. Can you suggest the most appropriate sector for it?

A Beneficial sectors in which to sleep or rest are the northeast, north, and east. Your head should be at the west or south end of the hammock when you lie down, since it is believed that, when you wake you should face north or east to gain from the good energies that originate there.

Q My house faces northeast. At the back, in the southwest sector of my garden, I have a water fountain. Is this an appropriate sector for water in Vastu Shastra?

A The water element belongs to the north sector, while the southwest sector belongs to the earth element. It is better to have a rock feature than a water feature in the southwest. You could drain the water from the fountain and substitute some rocks and pebbles of different shapes, colors, and sizes.

Q My back garden is T-shaped. What should I do about this awkward shape?

A You could fence off the two areas using hedges and shrubs. In Vastu terms, this would mean that you have two separate gardens, which should be treated as separate entities. You can then use a mandala to plan the garden layout according to the compass sectors, i.e., north, south, east, west, and so on.

Q What color of flowers should I plant in the different sectors of my garden?

A According to Vastu Shastra, each direction is ruled by an element, a color, a shape, and so on. If you want to build or design your home or garden along Vastu Shastra principles, you must observe the rules and follow the formulae as far as possible. While it is useful to recognize the specific sector colors, having other colors in each sector is not a problem, although it is best to let the sector color dominate.

Q I have a dog that sleeps in a kennel in my garden. Should I keep the kennel in a particular sector?

A You can keep the kennel in any sector other than the center or northeast of the garden, since the center is ruled by Lord Brahma and the northeast section is "the gateway to gods." You need to keep these sectors free from objects or furniture as far as possible to gain from the positive energies that emanate from these areas.

Q My neighbours have a swimming pool to the south of my garden. Is it bad luck to have water in this direction?

A The element of water belongs to the north sector, and the recommended area for a water feature is the north, not the south. If you can see the swimming pool from ground level, then you could build a tall fence in this area of your garden; if you cannot see it, then its effects will be minimal. But remember that the water is neither on your property nor within your mandala grid.

Q I have a fish pond in the north of my garden. Is it essential to have a certain number and a particular color of fish in my pond?

A I think you might be confusing Vastu Shastra with feng shui. In the latter, each direction is ruled by an element, a color, a shape, and a number. To enhance the luck of a particular direction, you can use any of the above in a feature. Hence feng shui recommends having a specific number of fish in a pond. Do not mix the two practices. Follow whichever you are comfortable with, but don't try to combine them.

Q I live in a studio apartment. How can I incorporate the earth element when I don't have anywhere to grow plants?

A Vastu Shastra considers that each of the five elements (fire, earth, air, water, and space) has to be present for harmony to exist. If you don't have sufficient space, you don't have to grow plants to incorporate the earth element. You can use fresh flowers, or even silk or paper flowers to beautify a room. Any object belonging to the earth element will do: even an earthenware vase, pebbles, or shells.

9

VASTU IN THE WORKPLACE

Optimum Vastu Shastra in the workplace is particularly difficult to achieve since the vast majority of us have little or no control over matters such as the part of the building in which we sit, or even in which direction we face. In this chapter, I will deal with the realms of what is ideal. Even if you have your own business, there are going to be some things that you can do and some that you can't. Likewise for people who are employees, although there will be a surprising amount of things that they can do. But, of course, there will probably be many more over which they have little control. However, there is one thing which everyone—from the most humble functionary to the head of the company—can do. It is a fundamental of Vastu Shastra—clear clutter! Whether you work in an office, a factory, or a store, stick to these principles: things that are wanted, but are not currently being used, should be stored away; things that are wanted and are in use should be kept neatly; and things that are unwanted altogether should be disposed of as soon as possible.

As a happy employee, you may be enjoying what you do at

above *North is the ideal direction to face for people doing any work involved with finances.*

left *A cluttered table is not conducive to good, creative work. Keep only things that are needed on your worktable.*

above *A room that is comfortable, well lit, and cheerful is conducive to work, encouraging output and hence profits.*

below *A plant can enliven dead corners or spaces in an office.*

work, but if, on the other hand, you are feeling lethargic or listless in your job and have started to make mistakes, or your work output is lower than what you think it should be, then it is time for you to take a look at your environment. Perhaps, on the other hand, you are the boss and you feel that your business is going well, but it should be going even better. You may feel that your business would improve if only you didn't have to cope with unnecessary and needless frustrations. You may feel, and even know, that your company is the best in the business, but still be asking yourself why you are not achieving your targets. Why are you spending your days surrounded by unhappy, bickering employees? Of course you must start by re-examining your business right down to its first principles, but also spare some time for an assessment of the premises according to Vastu Shastra principles.

Your office might be a room in your own home or it could be a whole floor of a building or even an entire building. Maybe you are planning your office space, or perhaps it is already built and operational. Whatever the building and whatever the nature of your business, you can apply the principles of Vastu Shastra to that space, for the benefit of the owners and all those who work there. Whether full-time or part-time, everyone can gain from Vastu Shastra. Improving the environment can bring many gains, financial and emotional, and might even improve efficiency and cut working hours.

Because we spend so much of our life and so many of our waking hours in our work place, the layout of that work place becomes as essential as the arrangement of our home. A good comfortable work environment enhances the health and thus improves the productivity of the staff. A harmonious environment can lead to more and better growth; it can bring general well-being to the staff members, to the company as a whole, and to the community in which the company is located. If the layout of the office is inauspicious, it can increase stress for the staff and lead to sickness and absenteeism, which will affect the productivity of the rest of the staff, the company profits, and ultimately the welfare of the greater community.

Vastu Shastra maintains that it is important for objects and people to be located in places most suitable to the elements and compass. Of course, you don't have to spend your whole life facing one direction, but you should be aware at all times of the optimum. By doing this, you will increase the flow of good energy and thereby contribute to the well-being of everyone living or working in this space—however big or small it may be.

below *Your work place should be fairly relaxed and happy so that you can concentrate on your job, which may have enough pressures of its own.*

ENTRANCE

The entrance to the property is very important. It should be well protected and looked-after. Vastu Shastra believes that a property or building should have two gates—one for entry and the other for exit. These should be staggered and not in a straight line. If the property opens directly onto the street—as is usual in big cities—then there should be a separate in-door and out-door, even though they may be on the same side of the property.

The outside area, near or around the main entrance, should be kept clean and clear—as for the private house, there should not be any potholes, stagnant water, or garbage near or around the gate. Even if the area outside the gates is not owned by the owner of the property, there is often little to stop the property owner from maintaining it The name of the company should be displayed prominently and above eye level so that it can be easily seen, and the company logo should be visible. At night-time, the company's name should be illuminated, if it is allowed .

above While revolving glass doors feature in many large office buildings, they are bad Vastu Shastra because they stop the flow of positive energy.

above The entrance to this building is big, attractive, and well lit. It is strategically placed on the main road, making it easily accessible and noticed.

117

If there are trees in the grounds of the building, they should be trimmed and not dwarf the office or building by their size or proximity. Gates or doors should open inward to the building or site. There should be no obstruction, such as a tree, lamppost, pillars, or pylons, immediately opposite the entrance. The gates or doors should be well looked-after and should not creak or make any protesting sounds when opening—hinges should be well oiled and the doors should be well painted and cleaned regularly. If there are tarnishable metal fittings, such as brass, they should be polished regularly and not left to go dull. If the doors are glass, they should be cleaned regularly, even daily.

Ensure that washroom doors do not face the entrance. If there are plants near the entrance, keep them watered, well-fed, and remove all dead leaves regularly. An office that has its main entry facing north, northeast, or east is preferable. A water feature, such as a fountain, not only enhances the appearance of an office but is also believed to help improve the finances of the company.

The entry hall does not have to be glitzy. It must, however, be kept clean, free of clutter, and inviting. Fresh flowers can be displayed in the lobby. They are attractive, and will improve the office's positive energies. If there is a color appropriate to the sector, then that color should be present in the decor, for example yellow for a south room or blue for a north room. In India reception areas of offices are adorned with images of gods or religious verses—this is done to seek their blessings. If the building has a basement, it is better that this space is not used as an office. Basements are considered most suitable for storing items such as stationery or old records.

above A colorful bunch of fresh flowers in a lobby or a reception area adds color and looks attractive.

above A water feature in the center of a building or in a courtyard is not good Vastu. The center should be kept open and free.

SHAPE

The preferred shape for the office, as for most buildings, is either square or rectangular. If the property is irregularly shaped, you can try re-configuring it to create two or more square shapes by using plants, furniture, screens, or partitions. Although it might be considered boring, the best arrangement inside the building is one that features "squared up" offices and work-stations. Frequently, this type of arrangement provides the most efficient use of space, which is often one of the significant cost factors in city center offices.

DOORS AND WINDOWS

The entrance doors into a building should always be bigger and more imposing that any of the interior doors in the office. The entrance doors are the "funnel" through which people and many of the energies come into the building, so do not restrict them in any way.

A door which faces the north, northeast, and east is more preferable than doors in the west, northwest, or southwest. If the door does not face one of the preferred directions see if there is any appropriate alteration that can be made so that the door will face a preferred direction. Perhaps the entrance could be at a slight angle to the face of the building. The door should not be located in the precise cardinal positions—0°, 90°, 180°, or 360°. If your building is so aligned that the morning sunlight falls at the main entrance, it is considered to be very auspicious. If the office is to be built anew, then consider specifying that there should be a lower level in the northeast so that the positive energies can collect there before they meander to the rest of the office. At

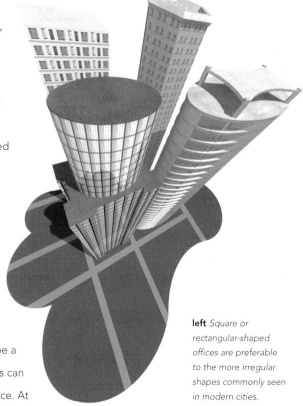

left *Square or rectangular-shaped offices are preferable to the more irregular shapes commonly seen in modern cities.*

119

the same time, specify a higher area in the south, west, and southwest of the office. Your architect should be able to accommodate both of these requirements without leaving any tripping hazards.

If the office in which you work is not air-conditioned and noise or dirt is not an issue, then any windows in the north, east, or northeast should be kept open as much as possible. Windows in the south, west, and southwest should be kept closed as much as possible.

above *Try to position your desk so that you are facing east while working.*

CORRIDORS

Long corridors are often a feature of offices; energies will rush through them at great speed, so use plants, lights, or pictures to slow the energies down. The corridors should be kept well lit.

right *Use simple and light furniture in the northeast sector of any office, house, or room.*

FURNITURE AND EQUIPMENT PLACEMENT

Position all furniture so that it does not restrict the free flow of energy. The heavier furniture, such as filing cabinets, shelves, and so on, should be placed in the west, southwest, and south of the room, or floor of the office building. The northeast should, as for houses, be free and lightly furnished as far as possible—again, this can be applied to the individual room, partitioned-off area, or even the floor of the office building.

below *The center of this office is free from any furniture and some staff face north. Those who face east when working will get the best of the energies.*

left This is a typical office, which has not been designed according to Vastu Shastra principles. The tightly-packed work stations look cramped and uncomfortable.

ROOMS

One of the trends in modern offices is to improve space utilization and communication between staff members by having fewer rooms and a more "open plan" approach, with staff occupying cubicles. In most cities, office space is expensive and at a premium, so it is a hard decision to leave the middle space in these congested areas open and free from any furniture. But if you are interested in incorporating the Vastu Shastra principles, then this is one of the most important criteria to specify for the design and the layout of the office. Many new offices now have an atrium in the center of the building, around which everything else is arranged. Although one of the perceived benefits of the atrium is light and spaciousness, it also provides the clear center of the building, which is so important in Vastu Shastra beliefs.

Many older offices, however, do not have this feature, and are dominated instead by rows of work-stations. Many people find it slightly unsettling when they have to work with their backs toward the rest of the room. Try reviewing the office layout and see if there is some way that everyone can be placed around a central open space. This need be only a token space; it is sufficient that you are respecting the principles of Vastu Shastra.

As for the building, it is always preferable to have a square room or office, rather than an odd or irregular shaped room. If you have a room that is L-shaped, U-shaped, or any other odd shape, then rearrange your furniture to create one or more square areas. Whatever type of building you are working with, you will probably need to make compromises as you look at your layout—cable runs and power outlets will inevitably influence your design.

LAYOUT OF INDIVIDUAL ROOMS

For each room, draw a plan of the layout, including the furniture, windows, doors, and so on, and place the Vastu Purusha Mandala over the plan. You can then match the grid square identifying which feature is in what compass direction.

NORTH

Lord Kubera, who governs wealth, health, and general well-being, rules the north. Facing north and being in the north is recommended for people doing any kind of work where they are dealing with finances—so this is the zone that is considered to be the best for people whose work is directly involved with the finances or financial health of the company. Their work-stations should be placed in such a way that they are facing north when working. This is also considered the best Vastu Shastra location for a safe, but care should be taken that it is well-protected. The safe should be located in such a manner that when the safe door is opened it faces north (i.e., the opening itself will not face north). Any confidential or secret documents, or papers important to the company, should ideally be kept in this location. Because the ruling element for this direction is water, try to incorporate any water feature, such as a drinks machine or water fountain, here. Any shade of blue would be a good color to use here, but remember, pastel shades are less overpowering.

EAST

Indra, the god of power, and the element fire rule here. This is a good general direction for anyone to face when working, since it is considered to be the source of enlightenment. East is where the sun rises and it is believed to bring positive energy to the office.

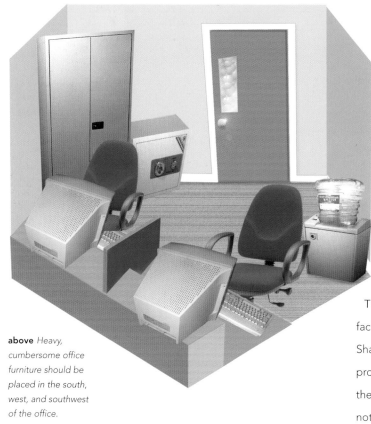

above *Heavy, cumbersome office furniture should be placed in the south, west, and southwest of the office.*

left *The north is ruled by the god of wealth, and is therefore the ideal place for a safe. It is also a good area in which to do financial or accounting work.*

This sector of a room should be more lightly furnished than others, if it is practical. In the overall plan of a building, east is the best location for any meeting room for the employees in general or for a conference room, since this is considered to be the most inspirational of all directions. If the company has a group of employees who are engaged in creative work, this is also the best place for them to be located. You can incorporate the color red in the soft furnishings, in pictures, images, and the overall decor. Once again, paler shades will be less overpowering than deeper shades.

above *East is an ideal sector for a meeting room or conference room. The table should be either square or rectangular in shape.*

below *Filing cabinets and cupboards should be placed in the south, southwest, and west. Lighter furniture should be placed in the north, northeast, or east.*

WEST

Although Lord Varuna, the god of water and rain, rules here, the element ruling the direction is, in fact, air and the direction color is gray. This sector in an office is the preferred area for locating senior executives and more senior staff. The gray color can be incorporated in the carpet color or any of the soft furnishings.

SOUTH

Lord Yama, the lord of death, duty, and responsibility, rules here. The element earth and the color yellow rule this zone. This sector of a room or building is the place where you should locate heavier items such as heavy desks and cabinets, so that their weight presses down on the negative energies. This sector is considered to be appropriate for someone who has or holds a senior status and position in the office – for example, an executive director. His desk should be placed in the south or west sector of the office and he should face north or east when working or meeting other people. A crystal vase, or maybe one made of porcelain or earthenware can be placed in this corner, or you could hang a picture that is predominantly yellow here to connect with the earth element.

NORTHEAST

This is the most auspicious of all directions, and harnessing these energies is believed to be most important if you wish to bring good fortune and good luck. This direction and sector is the gateway to the gods and is ruled by Ishanna, the god of purity. It is imperative that this sector is kept free of any clutter, dirt, and dust. It should be sparsely furnished. The positive energies will always pool here first and then spread to the rest of the office—furniture placed here is considered to adversely affect the good luck, wealth, and health of the office or the company. In an office, this sector is considered to be ideal for a reception area. If possible, you should design this part of the office so that it is a little lower than the rest of the office floor level. If your office has the space, this sector would be the one in which to build a common room for the staff where they can unwind, relax, or have a cup of coffee.

above *It is a good idea to locate a common area, where staff can take a coffee break, in the northeast sector of the office.*

below *The southeast sector of the office is the ideal location for the copier machine.*

SOUTHEAST

Agni, the god of fire, rules here. It is the best location for any electrical equipment, such as air-conditioning equipment, boilers, generators, LAN equipment, and so on. It is also a good place for a kitchen. Try to have the units positioned in such a way that whenever anyone is working at, or on, the equipment they will be facing east. In any room in the office, try to place phones, computers, faxes, printers, photocopies, etc. in the southeast sector.

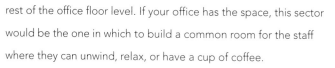

SOUTHWEST

Niritti, the god of misery, rules here, but this does not make this a bad or unfortunate zone. The sector is ruled by our ancestors and it is the place where the owner or chief executive officer should have their office. By being seated in this sector, it is believed that they will gain wisdom and strength and be fair, considerate, and just—all of these qualities are bequeathed to them by their ancestors. Leadership qualities are also believed to be enhanced here, too. The decisions that people make here are considered to be ones that will bring benefit, not only to the company as a whole, but also to its employees.

NORTHWEST

Vayu, the god of wind, rules the northwest section. Consequently, it is the recommended place for the marketing department to be. If the company is a trading organization, which "moves" goods, then this is also where the "goods" section should be located. Wherever there is a need for selling finished goods, the northwest is the location most associated with quick movement.

CAR PARK

The car park should be located away from the main office building. If the car park is a building, it should not be attached to the main office building, but stand at least a few feet away. Try to avoid locating the car park to the northeast section of the building—this section is the gateway to the gods and should be kept free, particularly of heavy vehicles and the fumes that go with them. Underground parking is not recommended since it is believed that it creates restless energies and is not conducive to the well-being of the people who work above this space. Although it is the norm for so many buildings, it is better to avoid the situation where you can.

right *A small office that is built between two overpoweringly tall buildings is not good Vastu Shastra.*

below *An office car park would be ideally located in the northwest section of the office site.*

125

VASTU IN THE WORKPLACE

10
QUESTIONS
& ANSWERS

Q We would like to use Vastu Shastra principles in the office. The problem is that it is an open-plan office. How do we establish the center?

A Ideally, the whole plot should be divided into nine equal squares. The middle portion is then considered the center. If you are lacking space, try to make a token space at the center—its size is not important, a gesture would suffice.

Q I am a fashion designer and have a workshop in which I and two other designers work. Which is the best sector for us to work in?

A All three of you have creative occupations, so the east sector of the workshop would be best. The god of power and enlightenment, Lord Indra, rules this section and would be beneficial to you. You should also try to face east while working—arrange your work area so that you can all face this direction.

Q I have my own business on one floor of a building that is not owned by me. How can I incorporate Vastu Shastra principles there?

A Place the Vastu Purusha Mandala on the floor plan of your office and designate each sector according to the mandala. If this isn't practical, then take each individual room and place the mandala on top of its plan and then design that room accordingly. Don't forget the outside of the building; make sure that the elevator and fire escape areas are as clean and tidy as the rest of your space.

Q I work mostly from home, designing websites, and the room that I use as my office is in the east sector of my house. Which is the best section of the room for me to sit and work in?

A The east sector of the house is very beneficial for you because east is the most inspirational direction. Your computer and other equipment should be placed in the southeast, which is a good area for electronics. You should try to face east when you are working or talking business on the phone.

Q I am choosing a new office. What is more important in Vastu Shastra: the entrance to the building or the entrance to my own particular unit?

A If you can, try to find a building that faces north, east, or northeast and then get a unit that faces this direction too. You want the best of all worlds if possible. Try to work within your budget—you might have to compromise and settle for one or the other, if the prices are too high.

Q I have a sunken water feature located in the center of my office. Should I get rid of it?

A Ideally, the center of any living space should be kept clear. Drain the water and raise the center, so that it is level with the rest of the office. Get your builder to give you some advice: you will need to do a proper job so that the water feature is made safe.

Q I am designing a 75-room service apartment in a building that faces east. I need to design an indoor swimming pool and the owners are keen on building a water feature at the entrance. What advice can you give me?

A The swimming pool should be located in the north sector of the hotel, since this sector belongs to the water element. The east sector is ruled by the fire element. If the owners want a water feature in the east, then you should design a "flowing" water feature, with the water running from west to east.

Q Where should I stand to take compass directions: inside the entrance of my office looking out, or outside the office looking in?

A The direction of your property is important in Vastu Shastra. If you are designing a house, you need to stand inside the property looking out in order to take directions. You will get a feel of the direction and location of each room by doing this and will also know where to place the mandala, once you have located the northeast section.

Q I own a beauty salon. Where should I locate my cash till, and where should I keep the handmade cosmetic products that I sell?

A You should place the cash till in the north sector of the salon, as this is the most secure section. Keep cosmetics and other items that you want to sell in the northwest sector, which is recommended for finished goods. You should also give considerable thought to how best to display the cosmetics—Vastu Shastra will not make up for poor marketing.

Q I would very much like to have a water feature in the office, since I understand that it enhances wealth luck, but just don't have any room for one. Will this affect my wealth luck?

A You do not have to have a water feature to enjoy wealth luck. Hanging a picture of a water feature on the wall in the north sector of the office will suffice. But although Vastu Shastra can enhance wealth luck, you will still have to do your bit.

10

GOOD VASTU PRINCIPLES

For centuries Vastu Shastra has been a way of life for many people in India. Today, it is also becoming a way of life in the Western world—once the principles have been implemented and applied to the environment, it becomes a natural, everyday living process. When you walk into a house that has been built or designed with Vastu Shastra principles, you will feel calm and at ease. The house will have an air of comfort that no amount of luxuries or fine silks or rich furnishings can bring. It is not necessary to spend huge amounts of money on interior designers, furnishings, and fittings in order to create a home that is relaxing, soothing, and in touch with the great cosmos. The Vastu Shastra home will enhance everything that is good in your life, building up a positive state of mind and protecting you from, or at least helping to negate, any bad luck.

In the previous chapters, we have talked about a step-by-step method of designing your space, whether it is at home, in the garden, or at work, so that your life improves. In this chapter, we will discuss how we should go about maintaining and living within these spaces in our everyday life.

below *Bright attractive colors and objects create a happy environment and are essential in both homes and workplaces.*

right *Vastu Shastra is not just about the placing of furniture or the functions of rooms, it is intended to enhance the flow of energy. By organizing your office and home you can spend more time enjoying life.*

Although the origins of Vastu Shastra lie in India and the Hindu religion, we must recognize that Vastu Shastra does not have to be limited to a special country or a religious belief. It is a gift to our universe, which can be used for the benefit of all. You do not have to change your religion or accept someone else's, or even have a set belief, to practice Vastu Shastra. It is all about getting in touch with your surroundings by fine-tuning your personal awareness of nature and the environment.

In the twenty-first century, we are so caught up in the frenzy of meeting deadlines, achieving goals, and indeed just making a living, that many of us cannot distinguish the natural from the synthetic. Sometimes we forget to stop and actually look at what is around us. We are so hungry and exhausted at the end of the day that all we want is to eat an instant meal and slump in front of the TV, watching some mindless entertainment. We might wake up exhausted, hating our job, and dreading the office, but never have the time to stop and look at what is actually happening. The burden of responsibilities, financial and emotional, is overwhelming.

But Vastu Shastra is something that can fit in perfectly within the modern lifestyle, becoming a part of everyday life and making it better, easier, and more comfortable. Once you have applied Vastu Shastra principles, you do not have to adhere to any elaborate rituals, or engage in wholesale destruction of your present environment. Just by making a few minor adjustments, everything becomes easier, both for you and for the people who live and work in your space.

above *Life is about changes, nothing stands still, our homes change too as our children grow up and leave home.*

It is important in Vastu Shastra that you should maintain your property and continue to review it; perhaps, by taking a fresh look at your property, you will come up with some new ideas and approaches. Maybe your family is growing or you have an elderly relative coming to live with you. You may need to build an extension to your home. Try to think of the extension as an integral part of your property—not just as an add-on. If you build an extension, start by reviewing the whole property from basics—don't forget to use the Vastu Purusha Mandala. It is possible that some of the things you wanted to do earlier can now be accomplished, because you are increasing the size of your building. When you design an extension, don't forget the importance of some of the fundamentals that cannot be changed once built—windows and doors, bathrooms and plumbing, kitchens and electrical wiring.

We live in a modern age, and we must continue to take advantage of the benefits that science brings us. So when it is time to replace that washing machine, you don't have to go back to basics and decide to live in harmony with your environment by washing by hand instead! On the other hand, you can replace the machine with one that boasts the most environmentally friendly technology—not the one with extra gizmos, but the one that needs less energy and water during the wash. Living in harmony means being economical with precious resources, so remember when you are doing your wash to use the lowest effective water temperature, and when you are disposing of your old washing machine, don't forget to find out if it can be recycled instead of being crushed and becoming yet another wasteful part of landfill.

below *As our children leave so our parents return. The family members who live in one house vary as life moves on.*

left *When you are planning your kitchen, it is good Vastu to ensure that you install only energy-saving devices that are environment-friendly.*

left *We are all dependent on creature comforts. But our well-lit, well-heated homes eat up precious electricity. Try to make adjustments to your lifestyle—turn off a light here or there, and keep the heating thermostat a degree or two lower.*

Remember that the magic of electricity comes at a price—not just financial, but also at the cost of Earth's precious resources, as more and more of these are used to generate the electricity, which we largely ignore and sadly abuse. Ultimately, our power-hungry society is responsible for the environmentally disastrous impact of carbon dioxide on our atmosphere. So, using less electricity helps the environment (and saves money). How can you use less electricity? Firstly, turn off all those unwanted lights. You don't have to go the spartan route of having just one bulb in a room—illuminate the room to suit your tastes and comfort, but ask yourself if you really need to leave lights burning in rooms that you are not using. If there are security considerations, consider timer switches and passive infrared detectors for activating lights. What about the television and other audio-visual equipment? Leaving them on "standby" burns electricity, so why not switch them off completely when not using them? This has the added advantage of removing a potential fire hazard. If you have it, do you really need your air-conditioning on all the time? Climate control has become a familiar, unnoticed, modern comfort. Ask yourself if you could bear to set the temperature just a little bit higher. Try zoning your home so that unused rooms are not climate-controlled. How about the centrally heated home? Try reducing the set temperature by a couple of degrees; even this small change will pass largely unnoticed but will help the environment. You can also turn off heat in any unused rooms, but make sure you don't land yourself with a damp room! If you do any, or all, of these things, you will be helping your environment by using less electricity, extending the life of the equipment, and once more saving yourself money.

above *Windows are recommended in the north, east, and northeast sector of the house or room.*

left *Discard any old newspapers and books that you have finished reading, and that you do not want to read again.*

When replacing any electrical appliances, do try to replace with energy-efficient equipment, and do try to recycle—every little bit you do in these areas is an achievement, a great success that brings you closer to nature. Of course, getting maximum use out of any item is good Vastu Shastra. Maintaining good Vastu Shastra means that you should rethink your priorities. Before replacing any furniture, furnishing, equipment, or clothes, first ask yourself, "Why am I doing this?" Very often the answer will not be "Because it's broken and can't be repaired" or "Because it's worn out." More likely it will be "Because I saw something I liked better," or "Because there's a later fashion" or "I just wanted a change," and so on. Think thoroughly before you replace anything for these reasons. Is it really necessary? Only you can determine whether it is, but remember that living in harmony is about protecting Earth resources. Even if you do go ahead and buy the new item, then do try to recycle the old. Invariably the best recycling method is to give the old item to someone or some organization that can re-use it.

Fundamentally, maintaining good Vastu Shastra in your home starts with cleanliness and eliminating clutter. When you walk into your home, look at it with the eyes of a stranger. Is there any unnecessary, unused furniture in the room? Ask yourself if you need it. If the answer is "no," then recycle it. If you have pictures and ornaments that you want to enjoy, then keep them—but make sure that they are not obscured by other ornaments that you do not need. Clutter is very easy to accumulate, but often it is very hard to discard.

below *Do you really need to replace your comfortable old chair? Think carefully before buying new furniture just "for a change."*

above You can recycle old glass coffee jars and use them to store your herbs and spices.

Don't forget the newspapers and magazines that you can so easily accumulate and don't forget those items in the kitchen that you will never use or are well past their "best by" date. Cabinets can also be cluttered! Do you recycle those fancy coffee jars as spice/rice/flour containers—or do you junk them? Just give it a thought.

A clutter-free environment is fundamental, and a clean environment is another absolute must. Clean the rooms in your home regularly—do not wait for them to look dirty. Polish those things that need to be polished. Don't forget to keep the approach to your home tidy and pay regular attention to your garden—trimming hedges, branches, and trees, cutting back over active plants, cutting grass, raking leaves. Do your maintenance, both inside and outside, regularly.

below Oil bottles and jars need extra care and attention since any grease on the outside will attract dust, and dirt is not good Vastu Shastra.

right A well-kept house and garden will encourage the good health, prosperity, and luck of the individuals living there.

REGULARLY RE-ENERGIZING THE HOME

Keeping your home clutter-free and clean will ensure that it is a good place for the energies. Even so, you can also re-energize your home occasionally by washing hard surfaces—though not delicate ones—using a small amount of sea salt dissolved in water. This is believed to chase negative energies away.

To dispel any negative energies, try walking around your house with an incense stick—the best time of the day is early morning or after sunset. You can chant a "mantra" or say a little prayer or just invite positive energies into your house. You should start in the northeast sector of your house and walk all around, ending up where you started. You can also use a charcoal burner with frankincense, myrrh, or some other incense or herbs. Treat burners with care!

above Incense-burning is a great way of chasing away negative energies and stale smells. It will help to attract good and positive energies into your home.

THE HOME AS A SOCIAL CENTER

We have seen that the house has a most important role in the successful application of Vastu Shastra. The house is a home for all of the family and the different parts of the house have their different uses. The house should not be split up into different "territories" with a different place for each of its occupants. It is for the use, enjoyment, and companionship, of all, including visitors. Close interaction between family members should be encouraged, as it will bond them closer and help them to achieve and share the same values and objectives. With the exception of a few areas, most of the house is communal, for the use of all the family.

By fulfilling as many of the goals of Vatu Shastra as we can, we can grow together and learn to live in harmony with our environment, with nature, and with those we love.

THE NINE RASAS

Inevitably you will enhance the beauty of the house and improve the comfort of its occupants with items such as pictures, flowers, rugs, or carpets. You will choose these items because you find them attractive, or attach sentimental value to them—maybe they are family heirlooms, or simply evoke happy memories. The items you choose to adorn your home should evoke certain emotions, or rasa. There are nine rasas in total, but the first five are the ones that you should try to activate. The last four should be avoided:

Shringara love, joy, and happiness.

Hasya humor and fun.

Vira heroism and noble feelings.

Adbhuta awe and wonder.

Sahnta peace and calm.

Karuna sadness and loneliness.

Roudra anger and aggression.

Bhayamata fear.

Bibhatsa repulsion and disgust.

PLANETS AND DIRECTIONS

Sun	east
Moon	northwest
Mars	south
Mercury	north
Jupiter	northeast
Venus	southeast
Saturn	west
Uranus	southwest

PLANETS AND COLORS

Sun	dark red and orange
Moon	white
Mars	bright red
Mercury	green
Jupiter	yellow
Venus	white
Saturn and Uranus	black

ZODIAC SIGN AND THE RULING PLANET

Aries	mars
Taurus	venus
Gemini	mercury
Cancer	moon
Leo	sun
Virgo	mercury
Libra	venus
Scorpio	mars
Sagittarius	jupiter
Capricorn	saturn
Aquarius	saturn
Pisces	jupiter

PLANETS AND PARTS OF THE BODY

Sun	head
Moon	face
Mars	chest
Mercury	hips
Jupiter	abdomen
Venus	pelvis, sexual organs
Saturn	thighs
Uranus	feet

PLANETS AND ELEMENTS

Sun	fire
Moon	water
Mars	fire
Mercury	earth
Jupiter	space
Venus	water
Saturn	air
Uranus	air

THE PLANETS AND THE PURUSHA

Sun	soul of the Purusha.
Moon	senses and emotions
Mars	power and strength
Mercury	rational mind and speech
Jupiter	knowledge and fortune
Venus	desire and yearnings
Saturn Uranus	sorrow and misfortunes

GOOD VASTU PRINCIPLES

10 QUESTIONS & ANSWERS

Q My partner has some ornamental swords and daggers that he likes to have on display. Does this go against Vastu principles?

A From a Vastu Shastra point of view, it is not beneficial to have such weapons displayed. However, since there are two people living in your house, the wishes of both of you need to be met. Discuss the issue with your partner, telling him how you feel. Perhaps, if he refuses to get rid of them altogether, you could settle on keeping them in one room—perhaps the basement, if you have one.

Q I am really taken by the ideals of Vastu Shastra, but I like to have pictures of Buddha in the house. Is that permitted?

A There are nine different types of rasa, or emotion—of which only five rasas are recommended. A picture of Buddha is inspirational and is one of the recommended rasas. Although you don't have to believe in any particular religion in order to practice Vastu Shastra, if you do, then bring it into your home—it can only be of benefit to you.

Q Which fragrance should I use in my incense burner, according to Vastu Shastra?

A Vastu Shastra does not specify a particular fragrance—as long as it is pleasing to you, that is all that matters. You can use any type of incense (provided it is legal). It could be one of the stronger aromas, such as frankincense, or a milder fragrance, such as jasmine; it alll depends on your own preferences and mood.

Q I have a large house with two bronze elephants at the southwest entrance. Does this fit in with Vastu guidelines?

A Elephants were originally used on ceremonial occasions for their presence and overpowering size, or at entrances as "ceremonial guards." The southwest sector of the house is ruled by the ancestors and the lord of misery, Nirritti. It contains the earth element, and having any object here that belongs to the earth element is auspicious. The sheer size and weight of elephants at your entrance will keep negative energies at bay. It is an excellent location for them.

Q My mother wants to buy me a dishwasher for my birthday. Is having such a piece of equipment in keeping with Vastu principles?

A There is nothing wrong with owning labor-saving devices. It is the misuse of them that is dubious. For instance, if you only have a couple of cups and saucers to wash up, then you might wash them by hand, or wait for a full load before switching on the dishwasher. Just suggest to your mother that she buys the most efficient machine that her budget will allow.

Q I believe in Vastu Shastra, but my parents do not and I live with them. How can I convince them to rearrange their living space in line with its guidelines?

A You should not try to impose your beliefs on them. You can probably rearrange your own room or space along Vastu principles without imposing on your parents. Simply plan the layout of your room using a mandala and then act accordingly.

Q I have an old, broken silver chain that I cannot bring myself to get rid of since it was given to me by my grandmother. Its value is purely sentimental. According to Vastu Shastra, can I display it and, if so, where?

A If the chain brings you joy and happy thoughts, do not get rid of it. Polish it, clean it, and display it proudly in the southwest or south sector of your house or room. The southwest is ruled by the ancestors and the wisdom that we can gain from them; and the south, justice and courage. So either sector is auspicious.

Q I want to keep my home fresh and nice-smelling, but can't afford to buy fresh flowers or expensive bottled aromas. What would Vastu Shastra recommend?

A Take a bowl of water and the petals of a few fragrant flowers such as roses. Place the petals on the water. This need not cost a lot, as you can buy just one or two flowers at a time. Your house will now smell fresh and fragrant.

Q Circumstances have been such that I have had to move to a very dilapidated neighborhood. How can I make the most of my situation?

A Your new overall environment might not be the best, but you can try to improve the inside of your home. Using the mendala, plan the layout of your house—and don't forget to do the same to your garden.

Q If I don't follow Vastu Shastra principles, am I going to have a tough time in life?

A Vastu Shastra is all about living in harmony with nature and your environment. It is not merely a passing fad, but has been around since the sixth or seventh century in India (although only recently in the West). If you believe in it and want to welcome it into your life in designing the layout of your space, that is great, since it can only bring positive results. If you don't believe in it and don't want to use it, that is your choice—your world will continue.

Glossary

AGNI Is the Vedic god of fire and rules the southeast direction. He is believed to be present in every home and is witness to every ritual. Agni is believed to have three forms: on Earth as fire, in the atmosphere he appears as lightning and in the heaven he manifests himself as the golden Sun.

ARTHA One of the four Hindu philosophies of life. Artha means action—it is goal oriented.

BRAHMA Is the four headed supreme creator of the world. He is believed to reside at the center of every home and office. Hence in the practice of Vastu Shastra it is essential that the center of the house is clear and empty.

DHARMA One of the four Hindu philosophies of life. Dharma means duty or responsibility.

DIWALI The festival of light that is celebrated in India every year in October or November.

INDRA Is the Vedic god of power and rules the east direction. He is a peaceful, heavenly ruler who offers protection to everyone who does their dharma, or duty.

ISHANNA Sometimes called Ish. He is the Vedic god of purity and rules the northeast direction.

KAMA One of the four Hindu philosophies of life. Kama means physical and material needs and desires.

KUBERA Is the Vedic god of wealth and rules the north direction.

MAHA BHOOTAS Or the five elements that are present in the universe. The five elements are Water, Earth, Fire, Air, and Space.

MANDALA Is a symbol of the universe and is square in shape, it usually has images of deities on it.

MANTRA Is a word or phrase that is chanted repeatedly when praying or meditating. A man can redeem himself by repeated chanting of this mantra. Surya is the benevolent god and his symbol is the swastika. There are three important temples dedicated to him in India and they are more than a thousand years old.

MOKSHA Is enlightenment. It is a blissful state and it means giving up any desires both material and physical to attain higher consciousness. To attain moksha is the main aim of every Hindu.

NIRITTI Is the Vedic god of misery and rules the southwest direction.

OM A sacred syllable which is intoned as part of the beginning and end of all rituals or prayers. Repeated chanting of this word is believed to lead to the creation of special vibrations and energy. This energy helps to connect an individual to the creator or the supreme being, who is the source of this energy. He helps the person to lose his or her individual identity and to merge with the source and become one.

POOJA Is the Hindi word for prayers.

PUNDIT A "pundit" is a religious and respected person. He officiates at ceremonies and rituals.

RASA Means emotion. There are nine rasas in all and the interior decoration of one's house should evoke one of the desirable rasas.

SHIVA Is the god of the five elements. In various parts of India there are temples dedicated to him and the five elements—there is the water temple, the earth temple, the air temple, the fire temple, and the space temple.

SURYA Is the Vedic god of the Sun. A special hymn or mantra is devoted especially in praise of the Sun. This is the holiest of the mantras in the vedas and is called the Gayatri

SWASTIKA In Sanskrit, the ancient language of India, "svasti" means well-being; "su" means good and "asti" means he is. Swastika, is an ancient Hindu symbol that was adopted by the Nazis in an inverted form. In India, it is a sign of good luck and is an emblem of the Sun.

VARUNA Is the Vedic god of rain and water and rules the west direction. He is supposed to be the protector of the fisherfolk who seek his blessings every time they sail.

VASTU SHASTRA "Vas" means to reside and "Vastu" means a place where people dwell. Shastra means body of knowledge.

VAYU Is the Vedic god of wind and rules the northwest direction. He is believed to have the power to purify the atmosphere.

VISHWAKARMA The divine architect who was mentioned in some of the earliest Hindu texts.

YAMA Is the Vedic god of justice, death and duty. He rules the south direction.

Further Reading

Books

Vijaya Kumar, *All You Wanted to Know About Vastushastra*, Sterling Publishers (P) Ltd,, 1999

Vibhuti Chakrabarti, *Indian Architectural Theory: Contemporary Uses of Vastu Vidya*, Oxford University Press, 1999

R. Venkatesh and Dr. S.L. Udaya Prabhakar, *Industrial Vastu*, The Avenue press, 1998

Bruno Dagens, *Mayamata*, Motilal Banarasidas Publishers, 1998

N.H.Saharabudhe and R.D. Mahatme, *Mystic science of Vastu*, Sterling Publishers Private Limited, 2000

Gayatri Devi Vasudev, *Vastu Astrology and Architecture*, Motilal Banarasidass Pub. Pvt. Ltd., 1998

Kathleen Cox, *Vastu Living*, Marlowe & Company, 2000

D. N. Shukla, *Vastu-Sastra*, Munshiram Manoharlal Pub. Pvt. Ltd, 1993

Narsiingh Lal Bansal and Deepak Bansal, *Vastu Shastra. Day-to-day use*, B.R. Paperback, 2000

Juliet Pegrum, *Vastu Vidya*, Gaia Books, 2000

Kamlesh Shah, *Vastudeep: The ancient art of modern living*, Business Publications Inc, 1999

Alice Boner, Sadasiva Rath Sarma and Bettina Baumer, *Vastusutra Upanisad: The Essence of form in Sacred Art*, Motilal Banarasidas Publishers, 1996

B. B. Puri, Vedic *Architecture and Art of Living*, Vastu Gyan Puvblications, 1995

Useful Addresses

Organizations

Institute of Vedic Vastu
and Research Foundation
Dawa Bazar
Indore, India
www.ivvrf.com

Mystic India
Synagogue Street
Calcutta - 700 001
India

Websites

Marharishi Global
Construction
www.mgc-vastu.com

Vastu Living
www.vastuliving.com

Vastu Rachana
www.vasturachana.com

Vastu World
www.vastuworld.com

Vastu Energy
www.harmony000.org

Vastu Forms
www.boloji.com/vastu

Vastu Shastra – Science
and Architecture
sites.netscape.net/ravindradi
nker/homepage.htm

Vastu Correction
without Demolition
www.vastukalp.com

Vaastu Shaastra
www.vastushastra.org

Vastu
www.ads-vastu.com

Vastu Consultant
www.vastuconsultant.com

Bilkis Whelan can
be contacted at:
consult@bilkiswhelan.com
www.bilkiswhelan.com

Index

Acknowledgements

*I would like first to thank God and then my father.
A very special thank you to my husband Michael,
who is my life and my love, for his continuous love, support,
encouragement, faith, and belief in me. I want to thank him
for his invaluable time, patience, and help with this book!
A big thank you also to Sophie Collins, the Publisher, and
Georga Godwin, the Project Editor, for their assistance.*

PICTURE CREDITS

CORBIS pps: 6 Bojan Brecelj, 11L Lindsay Hebberd, 12B Michael Freeman, 15R David Arky, 20TR David Cumming/Eye Ubiquitous, 22L Lindsay Hebberd, 23BR Craig Lovell, 24TL Elizabeth Whiting Associates, 29TR Bruce Burkhardt, 36 Bob Krist, 39B Jeremy Horner, 41R Sheldan Collins, 61T Cydney Conger, 66TL Michael Boys, 67 Craig Lovell, 72B Brian Harrison/Kudos/Elizabeth Whiting Associates, 75T Andreas von Einsiedel/Elizabeth Whiting Associates, 76TR Tim Thompson, 83T+85T Michael Boys, 87T Jerry Tubby/Elizabeth Whiting Associates, 88BL Rodney Hyett/Elizabeth Whiting Associates, 99T Lee Snider, 100BL Michael Boys, 101TR Ludovic Maisant, 102T+103BR+104L+105R Michael Boys, 106B+107TL Patrick Ward, 110B+111TL Eric Crichton, 118BR Roger Ressmeyer, 120B Rodney Hyett/Elizabeth Whiting Associates, 121 Kit Kittle, 124L Bill Varie, 130 Neil Lorimer/Elizabeth Whiting Associates, 131 David Bartruff

CORBIS/STOCKMARKET pps: 51R, 116B, 117T

THE IMAGE BANK/GETTYONE IMAGES pps: 18L Peter Turner, 19T Michael Melford Inc., 20ML Andreas Pistolesi, 44 Ross M. Horowitz, 65BR Ira Montgomery, 73R Farmhouse Productions, 77T Deborah Gilbert, 117B Double Exposure, 125B Harald Sund

FPG INTERNATIONAL/GETTYONE IMAGES pps: 27TL Justin Pumphrey, 33B Peter Adams, 39T+48/49 Peter Gridley, 50 Simon Bottomley, 57 Stephen Simpson, 74 Friedhelm Thomas, 80BL Rob Meknychuk, 90R Peter Gidely, 95T Rob Melnychuk, 98B Ken Ross, 123T Ron Chapple, 132TL Stephen Simpson, 133B Richard Price

STONE/GETTYONE IMAGES pps: 10R Mark Douet, 28TR Mark Lewis, 29BR Une Krejci, 35T Jamey Stillings, 37T Laurence Monneret, 38 Nick Daly, 94 B Stewart Cohen, 115T Danial Bosler

HUTCHISON LIBRARY: p22B

NASA pps: 27R ALL, 28L ALL, 29L ALL